SOCIAL SERVICES INSPECTORATE

BUILDING COMMUNITY SERVICES

The Mental Illness Specific Grant
A Review of the First Four Years

1991–1994

Written for SSI by	SSI Project Leader
Di Barnes,	Barry Norman
Centre for Applied	Inspector, Hannibal House
Social Studies	Elephant & Castle,
University of Durham	London SE1 6TE
	Tel: 0171-972 2456

Crown copyright 1995
Applications for reproduction should be made to HMSO's Copyright Unit
First published 1995

ISBN 0 11 321900 8

Previously published:
Planning into Practice: MISG Second Report on Monitoring its use 1991/92
(HMSO) ISBN 0 11 321586 X

CONTENTS

1.	**PREFACE**	1
	BACKGROUND	2
	THE THIRD MONITORING EXERCISE	2
	THE REPORT	3
	LANGUAGE AND STYLE	3
	ACKNOWLEDGEMENTS	4
	STUDY TEAM	4
2.	**SUMMARY**	5
3.	**KEY MESSAGES**	10
4.	**A REVIEW OF LITERATURE ON THE MENTAL ILLNESS SPECIFIC GRANT**	15
	INTRODUCTION	15
	ACHIEVING THE GRANT	15
	INITIAL IMPLEMENTATION—1991/2	16
	CONSOLIDATION—1992 TO 1994	18
	SUMMARY OF THE POSITION IN 1993	20
	1994/5 AND BEYOND	21
5.	**MISG ACTIVITY 1993/4**	22
	INTRODUCTION	22
	NUMBER OF PROJECTS	23
	MANAGEMENT OF PROJECTS, 1993/4	23
	NEW PROJECTS OR EXTENSIONS OF EXISTING ONES	24
	NATURE OF PROVISION	25
	OBJECTIVES	27
	WHO ARE THE PROJECTS FOR?	28
	NUMBER OF PEOPLE USING SERVICES	29
	EXPENDITURE	29
6.	**THE VIEWS OF MISG SERVICE USERS**	31
	SUPPORT AND UNDERSTANDING	31
	FRIENDSHIP	32
	GETTING OUT	33
	SHARING MEALS AND CELEBRATIONS	34
	TALKING	34
	WORKERS	35
	OTHER	35
7.	**ASPECTS OF GOOD PRACTICE**	37
8.	**PLANNING AND MANAGEMENT ISSUES**	48
	FINANCIAL PLANNING	48
	STRATEGIC PLANNING	49
	OPERATIONAL PLANNING	51
	INTERAGENCY ISSUES	54
	USER INVOLVEMENT	61
	QUALITY AND MONITORING ISSUES	63

9.	CONCLUSIONS	65
	PROJECT STUDY 1: DAY CLUB FOR ADULTS IN THE INDEPENDENT SECTOR	67
	PROJECT STUDY 2: VOLUNTARY SECTOR DAY CENTRE	70
	PROJECT STUDY 3: HOME BASED SERVICE	73
	PROJECT STUDY 4: HOME BASED SERVICE	76
	PROJECT STUDY 5: GROUP FOR MINORITY ETHNIC WOMEN	80
	PROJECT STUDY 6: GROUP FOR PEOPLE EXPERIENCING LOSS	84
	PROJECT STUDY 7: HOSTEL FOR THE HOMELESS	87
	PROJECT STUDY 8: HOME BASED SERVICE FOR PEOPLE WITH DEMENTIA	90
	PROJECT STUDY 9: RESPITE CARE FOR PEOPLE LIVING WITH DEMENTIA	94
	PROJECT STUDY 10: DAY CARE FOR OLDER PEOPLE IN A RURAL AREA	97
	APPENDIX 1: METHODOLOGY	101
	APPENDIX 2: THE VISITS	103
	APPENDIX 3: MISG ACTIVITY	104
	APPENDIX 4: MISG EXPENDITURE	110
	APPENDIX 5: BIBLIOGRAPY	113

PREFACE

1.1 The Mental Illness Specific Grant (MISG) was introduced in 1991 to reinforce the policy established in 1975 with Better Services for the Mentally Ill, and to carry forward the objectives of the community care White Paper 'Caring for People'; that is, to develop a comprehensive network of health and social care facilities to enable people with mental illness to be cared for, and treated, locally in the community. The purpose of MISG was to improve and expand social care services for people with mental health problems.

1.2 The Care Programme Approach (CPA), which was introduced at the same time as MISG, aimed to prevent people with mental illness falling through the care net by ensuring that systematic arrangements are put in place for the assessment of their needs, and the provision of their care. In August 1993, further development to assist safe and effective community care for mentally ill people was announced by the Secretary of State for Health in a 10 point plan. This led to the introduction of fresh guidance in May 1994 on proper arrangements for the discharge of mentally ill people from hospital. It also encouraged the development of better information systems. Supervision registers were introduced in April 1994 to identify mentally ill people most at risk of harming themselves or others, and to ensure that they are given the highest priority for follow up and care.

1.3 Particularly welcome was the inclusion of mental health as one of the five key areas in the Health of the Nation White Paper, 1992. This has stimulated research and development, and increased awareness of mental health issues generally. MISG, through the services it funds, has a valuable contribution to make to the three primary targets; to improve significantly the health and social functioning of mentally ill people, to reduce the overall suicide rate and, in particular, the suicide rate of severely mentally ill people. *(DH/Home Office 1992)*.

1.4 Also in 1992, the 'Reed Report' was published on completion of a major review of services for mentally disordered offenders and recommendations were made for the development of a range of alternatives to custodial care, including court diversion schemes. Again, MISG is one of the sources of funding available for such developments.

1.5 Since its introduction, therefore, MISG has had an ever larger role to play in the implementation of mental health policy and to reflect this, the grant entered its fifth year of operation on 1st April 1995 with an increase of £10 million. This, together with a £1.3 million uplift for inflation, brings the total amount of MISG available in 1995/96 to £47.3 million—an increase of around 31.3% on the £36 million allocated in 1994/1995. The increase reflects, not only the continuing need for the grant, but also its success. Therefore, it is timely to examine what MISG has achieved, and what lessons can be learnt to ensure the best use is made of the funding in the future. The 1994 monitoring of MISG set out to address these issues, taking as its focus the views of people using services supported by the grant. This publication reports on the findings.

BACKGROUND

1.6 MISG is a revenue grant, paid to local authorities, and ring fenced for spending on social care for people with mental illness, including dementia. The initial aim of the grant was to increase investment in community services for people in need of specialist psychiatric care. In addition, it now seeks to support the good practice and innovation already funded and to enable further growth of services targeting those most at risk, in particular people with severe mental illness.

1.7 When introduced in 1991, MISG was £21 million, £0.8 million of which was reserved for spending on the homeless mentally ill in London. The remainder was distributed to local authorities according to a formula based on the Personal Social Services Standard Spending Assessment (SSA). To access the grant, authorities have to contribute 30% to the cost of services from other sources. This meant that in 1991, MISG supported a total spend of £30 million. By 1993/4, the financial year covered by this monitoring, the grant had risen to £34.4 million in support of a total spend of £48.4 million.

1.8 The grant is available for services in the statutory and independent sectors but it may not be used as substitute finance for services already funded from other sources. It is, therefore, for new, or additional services, but once a service is set up using MISG, it can continue to be supported by the grant.

1.9 Local authorities have responsibility for the spending of MISG in their locality but must obtain the agreement of the district health authority. Decisions on how MISG will be spent must then be published annually in the Community Care Plan. The task of monitoring the use of the grant has been assigned to the Social Services Inspectorate (SSI).

THE THIRD MONITORING EXERCISE

1.10 This is third published report on the monitoring of MISG. The first monitoring exercise reported on the proposed use of the grant in its first year (Department of Health (DH/SSI, 1992): the second exercise reported on the actual use of the grant in 1991/2 (DH/SSI, 1993a). In 1992, the SSI also carried out inspections of selected MISG schemes in four local authorities (DH/SSI, 1993b). The following year, MISG monitoring was undertaken as part of a study by SSI into the impact of more general community care reforms on people with mental health problems (DH/SSI 1994a).

1.11 The 1993/4 monitoring relied on four sources of information:

- a review of literature—published circulars and reports of research and monitoring
- survey data obtained from local authorities
- visits by an SSI team to 10 selected local authorities
- follow-up visits by a researcher to seek the views of service users.

The survey was carried out between February and June 1994 and the visits took place between July and October (See Appendix 1 for methodology).

THE REPORT

1.12 The aim of the report is to:

- set the study in context with a review of the literature on MISG (Section 4)
- provide quantitative information on MISG usage and expenditure in 1993/4 (Section 5)
- record service users' perceptions of the projects they use (Section 6).
- highlight aspects of good practice identified by service users, staff and the SSI Team (Section 7)
- summarise the issues found to be arising from MISG in the authorities and projects visited (Section 8)

1.13 The report is written with the diversity of people involved with MISG in mind. Service users are central to the report and it addresses issues of practice as well as planning and management. Recognising that some readers will not wish to read the whole, it is divided clearly into sections and sub-headings are provided in the margin for easy referencing. Further detailed information and project studies are included in the appendices.

LANGUAGE AND STYLE

1.14 Important features of the report are the voices of service users and examples of practice found in MISG projects. To distinguish this information from the text, practice examples and illustrative material from MISG projects are placed in boxes and quotations are in italics. All quotations are from users unless otherwise attributed. To maintain confidentiality, names have been changed.

1.15 The use of the term 'service user' requires explanation. Many of the people participating in the study objected to the term, and many projects had had discussions on what term was more acceptable. One MISG project had held an open seminar on the subject but the discussion had been inconclusive. Preference was found for:

Preface

- member (of clubs, groups and day centres)
- client
- survivor

but no single term was found to be universally satisfactory. As a result, this report continues to refer to 'users' but, in acknowledgement of the wishes of participants, their preferred term is used when referring to their particular project.

ACKNOWLEDGEMENTS

1.16 The help and co-operation of the authorities in welcoming the SSI team, programming visits and providing paperwork was greatly appreciated. The team would also like to thank the users and workers in the MISG projects visited for their welcome, the openness with which they spoke and the trouble they took to make sure visits were useful.

STUDY TEAM

Diana Barnes	University of Durham
Julie Barnes	SSI Central Inspection Group
Reba Bhaduri	SSI HQ
Stuart Boyd	SSI Central Region
Margaret Clough	SSI Northern Region
Brian Cox	SSI London Region
Mary Hancock	SSI HQ
Christiana Horrocks	SSI HQ
Barry Norman	SSI Southern Region
Gary Smith	SSI HQ

SUMMARY

2

The report

2.1 This report presents the findings of the third monitoring of the mental illness specific grant (MISG) which was carried out between February and October 1994. The study differed from previous monitoring exercises as it used a number of sources of information; the 1993/4 official MISG returns on the use of the grant, reports of visits to local authorities and MISG projects made by a team from the SSI and a research study into the views of users. The result is a mix of quantitative and qualitative information aimed to attract a wide readership from the range of people involved in planning, managing, delivering and receiving MISG services.

Context

2.2 The review of MISG literature explains the origins of the grant and its role in the development of community care since its introduction in 1991. Although there were initial teething problems in the first year, these did not prevent the grant stimulating investment in a large number of projects regarded by service users to be beneficial. The principle issues raised by the first (DH/SSI,1992) and second (DH/SSI,1993a) monitoring were the difficulties in the way of using MISG strategically, the common perception that the grant was only short-term, and the lack of attention paid to recording and management information systems.

1993/4 usage

2.3 Analysis of the use of the grant in 1993/4 estimated there could be as many as 1,200 MISG projects nationally. The survey found that the management of MISG projects remained mixed, under half (49%) being in social service departments (SSDs) and 37% being run by voluntary agencies. Only a very small number were found to be in the private sector.

2.4 Diverse use was being made of the grant. Day care (25% of projects) and the provision of staff in mental health teams (21%) were the most common types of projects funded but, within these categories, there was considerable variation. The trend was towards very individualised care, often in the home, provided by outreach services, home support teams and individual support/specialist workers. The largest other categories of use were accommodation and employment schemes and services for carers. The accommodation projects (10%) tended to be providing opportunities for supported housing, the employment schemes (6%) largely prepared people for work, and the majority of the carers' projects (5%) were catering for the families of people with dementia. The number of users' projects (3%) was welcomed but investment in schemes specifically for mentally disordered offenders was disappointingly low.

2.5 The majority of MISG projects aimed to sustain people in the community and reduce hospital admissions, largely through the provision of support, be it domiciliary, social, emotional or practical.

Summary

The 13% of projects with the primary purpose of providing a safe and stimulating environment showed that building based activities were still important, although now in a minority.

2.6 Data on the number of people benefiting from MISG projects needed to be treated with caution but the 804 projects for which details were received, were reported to be benefiting over 31,000 severely mentally ill people under 65 and more than 19,000 older people. The projects were benefiting 14,500 carers, 6,500 people from black and minority ethnic communities, 5,250 people resettled for long stay hospital and 4,500 homeless people.

Expenditure

2.7 The number of local authorities which responded to the request for expenditure information was relatively low. Eighty authorities, including only two inner-London boroughs, submitted material for this part of the monitoring which covered the financial years 1992/3 and 1993/4. In these eighty authorities, there was an 18% increase in overall expenditure on services for mentally ill people from approximately £66.5 million in 1992/3 to approximately £78.5 million in 1993/4.

2.8 With regard to MISG, the total grant allocation for 1993/4 had been fully spent by 31st March 1994. In 1992/3, around 75% of MISG was spent on SSD managed schemes in the authorities providing information; services managed by the voluntary and private sectors accounted for some 20%. From 1992/3 to 1993/4, the trend in spending, though small, was away from SSD managed MISG projects and towards projects managed in the independent sector. The percentage spent on joint health and SSD managed projects remained roughly the same. Approximately four-fifths of authorities found their local 30% contribution towards MISG from base budgets with most of the rest coming from joint finance. This pattern was consistent over the two years being studied.

Finance

2.9 The proportion of total SSD expenditure spent on mental health was still found to be small in 1993/4, but, as reported, it was on the increase. The contribution of MISG to this expenditure continued to be welcomed. Although the annual uplift of the grant in 1993/4 had been equal to little more than inflation, this small rise eased the difficulties experienced by some authorities in financing their 30% local contribution. Some authorities expressed concern about the time limited nature of MISG and many agreed that there was a need to raise the priority of mental health in SSDs. Social services departments' information on mental health expenditure in general, and MISG in particular, needed improvement.

Users Voice

2.10 Looking within MISG projects—many of which were new and providing a service not previously available—service users identified that the aspects of the social care which they valued most were:

- shared support and understanding
- learning from each other
- meeting friends, getting out and being in company
- doing things together, taking trips and going on holiday
- the opportunity to talk, knowing it is in confidence
- gaining confidence and feeling more able to cope.

Good Practice

2.11 Staff were found to be generally highly motivated, the success of many projects being largely due to their skill and commitment. Service users who participated in the study, and members of the visiting team, highlighted interesting examples of good practice including:

- responsiveness to individual needs
- ready access 24 hours a day
- cultural sensitivity
- keeping an eye out for changes in people and responding appropriately
- working with risk
- working with other agencies
- involving service users
- involving carers and families
- providing transport for users in rural areas, with restricted mobility and for reasons of safety
- good information sharing
- staff supervision, support and teamwork
- a policy to ensure the safety of staff.

Strategy

2.12 Strategic planning in mental health remained slow to develop for financial and structural reasons resulting in incremental, rather than strategic, use of MISG. The grant has undoubtedly pump-primed new development arising from assessed needs but it has often been used to plug gaps in services without adequate consideration being given to broader strategic issues.

Operations

2.13 The MISG schemes visited showed a high level of compliance to the criteria laid down for the grant. Emphasis was found to be placed on hands on care provided in response to individual need to help maintain people at home. However, at project level, MISG was often not well understood and had no special identity. Projects also stressed the pressures that they experienced such as demand overtaking resources, high expectations placed on workers and volunteers, and anxieties that competition could lead to cost cutting which would adversely affect quality.

Interagency issues

2.14 Interagency work is integral to the grant and MISG has certainly continued to encourage joint planning. However, although consulted by LAs over the use of the grant, there was little evidence of health authorities influencing decisions on how the grant was to be used. On the other hand, the influence of the voluntary sector was considerable

Summary

		although the initial involvement of voluntary agencies tended to be reactive, in response to invitations to bid for MISG funds from SSDs. This tended to favour well established organisations but some new providers were found to be gaining confidence, often with managerial and developmental advice from the SSD.
CPA	2.15	The development of the care programme approach (CPA) and care management was found to have been warmly welcomed by MISG projects in authorities where the systems were working well. Particularly beneficial, for both service users and workers in projects in the independent sector, was the accessibility of, and support from, designated key workers and care managers. MISG projects had also benefited from access to care management budgets which enabled them to provide a more responsive approach to care needs of individuals. In authorities where CPA had not been implemented, and/or had not been clearly linked with care management, projects were experiencing confusion, and a deterioration of interagency working.
User involvement	2.16	User involvement was found to be commonplace in MISG projects with abundant examples of good practice and some investment of MISG in user groups. Many models are being adopted. The effectiveness of involvement was very difficult to judge at the levels of strategic and locality planning. Within projects, the process of setting up and running users' committees was often as important as the outcomes. Projects which had not involved users in the planning and running of the service, usually included feedback from users in their annual reviews.
Quality	2.17	Much more work was found to be required on the setting and measurement of quality standards. This work is just beginning and project staff reported increased use of, and demand for, service level agreements with clearly specified requirements for quality and monitoring. Monitoring remained unsystematic almost everywhere, and was often not carried out. Evaluation and review were also undeveloped; evaluations were ad hoc and reviews tended to be unstructured annual reports.
Conclusion	2.18	The third monitoring exercise found that MISG continued to support many innovative and pioneering projects which were contributing significantly to the provision of community care for people with severe mental illness. Gaps in services remain and issues around the planning and further development of effective community based mental health services need to be addressed, but MISG has the support of many of its service users:

"This project has meant meeting others with similar illness who understand what mental illness is. Unless one has suffered mental illness, can you fully understand the suffering and trauma one goes through being misunderstood by the public in general? This type of illness can happen to

anyone. Yes, even you. I was ignorant of mental illness. It couldn't happen to a fit man like me—yet it did. Thanks to this project, I along with the others attending, find peace of mind and help and understanding." **George**

KEY MESSAGES

3

3.1 **In 1993/4, the grant continued to stimulate development in a wide range of projects targeting adults, including older people, with severe mental illness.**

- The estimated number of MISG projects in 1993/4 could be as high as 1,200, showing a considerable increase on the 781 projects known to have been operating in 1991/2, the first year of the grant.

- The study found that the grant is being used to fund a wide variety of schemes. Almost half of the projects fell within the umbrella of day care services (25%) or mental health teams (21%) but the trend was away from building based services to innovative, outreach and home based schemes. The other principle types of MISG services were housing projects (10% of all projects) and employment projects (6%).

- 62% of projects targeted people with severe mental illness under the age of 65, and 36% of projects targeted severely mentally ill people over 65, but there was some overlap between these categories in projects which welcomed people irrespective of age.

- Other groups reported to be benefiting from MISG projects included families and carers (51% of projects), people from black and minority ethnic communities (34%) and people being resettled from long stay hospital (31%). However, in the survey carried out, only 5% of projects were for people from ethnic minority communities exclusively, but this figure might reflect to the very low response rate from London boroughs.

- Data on the number of people benefiting from MISG projects needs to be treated with caution. Estimates from the 804 projects included in the survey, however, suggested that over 31,000 severely mentally ill people under 65, and over 19,000 people older people, benefit from these services. The projects were benefiting 14,500 carers, 6,500 people from black and minority ethnic communities, 5,250 people resettled for long stay hospital and 4,500 homeless people.

3.2 **MISG projects were commended for their diversity, innovation and good practice by the SSI Team and the service users themselves.**

- The development of 24 hour services, home based services and ones responding to the individual, and changing, needs of users were particularly welcomed.

- Also welcomed were specialist services responding to needs such as those of people from minority ethnic communities, women, older people, carers, young people and people experiencing particular problems or illnesses.

- MISG projects have demonstrated that small services can be successful in supporting people with mental illness in the community.

- With experienced staff, effective support and supervision, and attention to safety, MISG projects were succeeding in supporting very ill people at home, using hospital admission only when appropriate.

- Widespread use of non-mental health professionals in MISG projects has led to the emergence of specialist, unqualified workers who were found to be highly motivated, and who, with regular supervision and support, were achieving encouraging results.

- Users, and the providers of care in the statutory and voluntary sectors were working towards developing an effective voice in the planning and running of projects. Greater difficulty was being experienced in developing effective user involvement at a strategic level.

3.3 MISG had contributed beneficially to the development of the mixed market of care but this had not been without problems.

- The voluntary sector has made very good use of the grant but few private agencies are providing MISG services. This may reflect the interest of the private sector in residential care, rather than day or home based care, for mentally ill people at the time of the main thrust of MISG spending in 1991/2.

- MISG has encouraged new partnerships between the statutory and independent sectors, and between health and social services, but there have been few jointly managed projects.

- Gaps in provision remained such as in services exclusively for mentally disordered offenders.

- Pressure on services caused by their popularity, and the extent of the need, created difficulties for many MISG projects. This had particularly affected services targeted towards people with long-term needs because the turn over of users was low. Problems included:
  - a loss of flexibility in the support given
  - over commitment of funding
  - unrealistic expectations on staff.

- When deciding how MISG was to be used locally, the type of service to be developed had been discussed and even researched but frequently inadequate consideration had been given to which agency, or sector, was best placed to provide the service, its commercial viability and potential for growth.

- Where alternative local services were competing for LA funding, the staff of MISG projects were anxious that quality should not be compromised by competition for its own sake. Cost cutting could seriously damage the quality of care in some MISG projects, for example, putting 24 hour access to the service, and the safety of users and workers at risk.

3.4 The ring fencing of MISG finance for spending on social care for people with severe mental illness remains crucial.

- The ring fencing of MISG has ensured the development and continuation of mental health services at a time of widespread economic difficulty and fundamental change.

- Although MISG makes up but a small proportion of social services expenditure on mental health, it has prompted many local authorities to increase, albeit modestly, the amounts they spend on mental health services from sources other than MISG, such as the Special Transitional Grant (STG) in spot contracting.

- Uncertainty over the future of MISG projects was engendered by the fact that the grant was often treated as a time-limited, temporary measure, and also by the widely held, but mistaken, belief that if MISG ceased the funding already allocated under the grant would be withdrawn. Local authorities needed reminding that in this eventuality, existing MISG funding would be subsumed within the normal funding of services through the Standard Spending Assessment mechanism. It might, therefore, cease to be ring-fenced for spending on mental health, but would not disappear.

3.5 The strategic use of MISG continued to be hampered.

- Despite MISG acting as a catalyst to encourage joint planning, jointly agreed mental health strategies had rarely been developed, and the statements of general direction which existed often lacked specificity on goals, measurable outcomes, time scales and responsibilities.

- Obstacles to the development of a strategic approach included:
  △ lack of a financial foundation
  △ difficulties in ensuring the participation of the stakeholders
  △ lack of assessment of need
  △ difficulties of working strategically with health.

- The influence of health authorities on MISG decisions was felt to be positive, but small.

- Local authorities' inexperience in planning the development of new services across sectors, together with the lack of strategic direction, was continuing to encourage opportunistic development.

3.6 **The overall quality of MISG service was good but attention needed to be paid to issues of monitoring and review.**

- Use of contracts and service level agreements was uneven:
  - quality standards in service level agreements were often not made specific, and tended to be limited to principles and good practice
  - in-house providers in SSDs were frequently not operating within service level agreements
  - neither service levels, nor standards of output, were specified in most spot contracts.

- MISG projects were subject to annual reviews but, even though many services were innovative, few had been evaluated.

- There was commitment to monitoring but little progress had been made towards setting up a systematic approach to information collection.

3.7 **CPA and care management enhanced the work of MISG projects in authorities where the systems were working well. The patchy implementation of CPA and the under development of links with care management in some authorities gave rise to concern.**

- The main advantages of CPA and care management identified by the LAs, MISG workers and services during the monitoring visits were:
  - CPA and care management gave project workers, users and carers easier access to professionals
  - systematic reviews were held at which project workers were able to act as advocates for clients
  - care management gave access to a budget which could enhance the care of people using MISG projects.

- Implementation of CPA remained patchy and the outstanding concerns were:
  - within projects there was found to be a lack of understanding of CPA and the role of keyworker
  - reports from some SSD staff that there was some resistance to implementation of CPA by psychiatric consultants.

- Issues which arose from the implementation of care management focused on the provider role of MISG projects in relation to the purchasing role of care managers and included:
  - the gap in social work provision left by mental health social workers moving over to be care managers—this placed increasing demands on workers in MISG services
  - the expectation that social workers would adjust to the purchasing role with little, or no, training
  - inconsistent access to care management budgets throughout local authorities

△ the importance of CPA and care management working together to ensure a consistent approach for care providers.

A REVIEW OF LITERATURE ON THE MENTAL ILLNESS SPECIFIC GRANT

INTRODUCTION

4.1 This literature review aims to set the 1993/4 national MISG monitoring exercise in its historical context and to summarise the published findings of earlier monitoring and research. Therefore, it examines the reasoning behind the grant, what the grant has achieved and the issues it has raised.

4.2 Being introduced in 1991/2, MISG has only a short history but, within this time it has passed through several distinct phases due to its developmental nature. The phases identified are:
- background to the launch of MISG
- initial implementation—1991/2
- consolidation—1992 to 1994
- 1994/5 and beyond.

ACHIEVING THE GRANT

4.3 MISG arose as part of the general concern surrounding the lack of progress being made in the implementation of the policy to close long-stay mental hospitals and to provide adequate, and appropriate, services for people with severe mental illness in the community (*DHSS, 1975*). The concerns were highlighted in the official reports published in the late 1980's leading up to the NHS and community care reforms (*SSI, 1991*). In particular, concern was expressed over:
- the lack of clear areas of responsibility for the provision, and reprovision, of services in the community for both people with mental illness who are discharged from hospital and for people who had never been in hospital, (*House of Commons, 1985; Audit Commission, 1986; Griffiths, 1988*)
- the lack of resources, including bridging finance, to reprovide health services outside the hospital prior to closure, and to provide social services (*House of Commons, 1985; Griffiths, 1988*)
- the inadequacies of inter-agency planning (*Audit Commission, 1986; Griffiths, 1988*)
- the small proportion of social service spending on mental health (*SSI, 1991*).

4.4 The first mention of a 'specific grant' targeted for people with mental illness was made in the Griffiths Report (1988, p18) which proposed that the grant would facilitate the transfer of responsibilities for care from health to social services. It would also be linked to collaborative service planning, and would help to ensure effective care management for individuals.

4.5 A Department of Health Working Party was set up to review mental health planning and provision in the Personal Social Services. It recommended a grant with 100% funding, initially for adults aged 16-65, but later extended to include older people (*SSI, 1991*).

4.6 MISG was officially announced by the Secretary of State for Health on 12 July 1989:

'On the social care side, we have decided to create a new grant directed at encouraging local authorities to make their necessary contribution to services in line with health authority plans and objectives.' **(Hansard, 1989, p 974)**

4.7 It was explained in Parliament (*Hansard, 1989*), and confirmed in the White Paper (*DH, 1989*), that the aim of MISG would be to increase the availability of community care services for the mentally ill. The issues of collaborative planning and care management were addressed by the requirement for MISG expenditure plans to be jointly agreed by health and social services authorities. This linked MISG closely with the health-led Care Programme Approach (*CPA*); the systematic assessment and follow up care of severely mentally ill people. Although CPA was not perceived as requiring any new services, it was recognised that, in responding to CPA, social services 'will have available specially targeted resources through the new specific grant which is to be used in ways agreed with relevant DHAs' (*DH, 1990a, p76*).

4.8 Final details of the grant were announced in September 1990 (*DH, 1990b*). £21 million was made available, to support a total spending of £30 million on social care services for people with severe mental illness.

INITIAL IMPLEMENTATION—1991/2

4.9 Overall, MISG was welcomed but with reservations (*Groves, 1991; Barnes, 1992*). The principle concerns expressed were:

- the small size of the grant to meet the multiple needs of resettlement from hospital, care in the community and homelessness (*Foster, 1991; Hudson, 1990; Hogman and Westall, 1991*).
- the short lead-in time for the submission of proposals which gave little time for adequate planning and consultation (*Barnes, 1992; Groves, 1991; Hogman et al, 1991; SSI, 1991*).
- the 30% contribution required from local authorities or other sources (*DH, 1991a; Cobb, 1990*).
- the short-term nature of the grant with ring fencing assured for an initial period of three years.
- the initial lack of capital to support the revenue spending (*Hudson, 1990; Groves, 1991; Hogman et al, 1991*).
- the danger of a medical bias being imposed on plans for social care because of the involvement of health authorities in grant spending approval (*DH, 1991a; Hogman et al, 1991*).

4.10 Despite these concerns, MISG achieved considerable success in its first year and some of the fears proved groundless. Instead, implementation brought new issues to the fore, and achievements often raised questions of policy and practice which required further work, time and investigation. Much of the information on this phase of MISG comes from three sources; the official monitoring carried out by the SSI (*DH/SSI, 1992 and 1993a*), a study of a sample of 14 local authorities undertaken for the National Schizophrenia Fellowship (*Hogman et al, 1991; Hogman, 1992*) and a three year study into the impact of MISG in the Northern Region carried out at Durham University (*Barnes, 1992*).

4.11 Although, undoubtedly MISG was a small amount of money when looked at against national figures on the cost of care for people with severe mental illness, SSI monitoring found that the grant enabled 781 'major' projects to be developed in the first year of the grant, and that the amount of activity generated was impressive. As community mental health services started from such a low base, this led to a significant improvement in provision, and a 21% increase in social service spending on mental health.

4.12 The 30% share of the grant expenditure which had to be raised locally caused problems for many local authorities which were facing large expenditure cuts and capping measures, but only one authority failed to apply for MISG, and a further two authorities failed to realise their plans. The signs were that authorities could have raised funds to support a much larger grant as bids for the underspend of £194,000 topped £1.25 million.

4.13 The short lead in time was found to make consultation difficult, particularly with service users and carers, but this was balanced by an increase in interagency planning and activity to ensure that the grant was spent

4.14 The main achievements in the first year were found to be:
- the number of new services set up, or old services extended
- the amount of innovation introduced
- the high proportion of the grant spent on direct service provision.

Analysis of the first proposals for spending MISG raised concern about the predominance of traditional services funded in the statutory sector (*Day, 1991*) based existing plans which were being brought 'off the shelf', and on existing buildings. However, the services which became operational during the year showed evidence of a substantial shift to the voluntary sector and to innovative, informal services. The benefit of these services was felt by some to be unproven (*Groves, 1991; Coia, McKillop and McCreadle, 1994*), but there was evidence that they were developed in response to suggestions from professionals, users and carers.

4.15 A significant issue for authorities was the spending of the grant within the prescribed time frame. Slippage in spending was universal, but many authorities spent the grant by either substituting plans, investing differently in their committed projects or supporting one-off projects. All the research found this spending to be in the spirit of the grant, but it did carry with it certain disadvantages. Substitution tended to be directed to organisations which were known and, therefore, discriminated against black and minority ethnic groups (*Day, 1991*). Also consultation was often absent, action was opportunistic and little attention paid to strategic plans.

4.16 There were a number of difficulties in the way of MISG being used strategically:
- the grant pre-dated Community Care Plans. Many authorities had no agreed strategy for the development of community mental health services
- social services authorities often covered a number of DHAs so adding to the complexity of joint planning. In addition, mental health NHS trusts were being introduced and the nature of joint planning was changing
- the involvement of service users and carers in the planning process was under-developed and, where it was attempted, it often took place alongside rather than within the strategic planning structures
- the short lead-in time discouraged consultation.

4.17 Other concerns, which were raised by examination of the performance of MISG in its first year, were:
- whether the MISG developments were successfully targeted at the severely mentally ill and older people with dementia
- the lack of financial information enabling the identification of social services spending on mental health
- the inadequacies of information on assessment of need
- the need for measurable outcomes, monitoring and quality assurance within projects.

CONSOLIDATION—1992 TO 1994

4.18 MISG was increased by 50% in its second year to £31.4 million to support total spending of £44.5 million for 'the continuation and expansion of services agreed in 1991/2, or development of new services' (*DH, 1991b and c*). In explaining the grant, reference was made to its relevance for 'homeless people whose seriously impaired social functioning is a consequence of mental illness'. The use of MISG to ensure the effectiveness of CPA was again emphasised (*DH, 1991d*).

4.19 The increase in the grant was welcomed, as was the extension of ring fencing by one year to 1994/5. This was particularly appreciated by services established on three year contracts which had experienced delays in starting in the first financial year of the grant (*Barnes, 1992*).

4.20 The boost to MISG funding added to the optimism created by the grant. The availability of resources, and the resultant activity, was having a very positive effect on morale (*DH/SSI, 1993b*) and a ripple effect was observed (*GPMH/SSI, 1993*). Inclusion of mental illness in the Health of the Nation Key Areas also helped to establish that 'something is happening in mental health' (*GPMH/SSI, 1993, p19*).

4.21 A number of aspects of the new MISG projects gave rise to this optimism:
- exciting, innovative approaches to the provision of services (Barnes, 1993 and 1994)
- the ingenuity used to get projects up and running quickly (DH/SSI, 1993b)
- new areas for development, especially projects with mentally disordered offenders (Hogman, 1992)
- the development of new partnerships between agencies and sectors and with users and carers (Barnes, 1994)
- gaining experience in different forms of contracting and in the use of flexible budgets (GPMH/SSI, 1993)
- the exploration of new practice issues such as dealing with confidentiality across the inter agency interface (GPMH/SSI, 1993; DH/SSI, 1993b).

4.22 The SSI inspections in 1993 concluded that there was clear evidence that:

'MISG funded projects have had a very significant beneficial impact on the lives of users and carers.' (DH/SSI, 1993b, p vii)

Users explained that the quality of their lives had been improved, their self-esteem enhanced and their reliance on other mental health services reduced. It was also found that projects had adopted principles which furthered the objectives of the NHS and Community Care Act such as independence, choice and personal control.

4.23 Some of the early concerns about MISG were still being raised but these were much more firmly placed in the context of community care implementation as care management, and the clarity of purchasing and provision roles, was becoming felt. The main concerns at this time were:
- **Planning.** Strategic planning for mental health services was still lacking and, although more involvement of users and carers was found in the planning process (*DH/SSI, 1993b*), effective involvement was sometimes hindered by joint planning structures (*DH, 1994a*). Also, it was recognised that high need groups, such as carers and black groups, had not become involved and needed encouragement. Good information systems and widespread consultation was needed to improve the identification of local needs

(*GPMH/SSI, 1993*). Carers were often missed from consultation around mental health and perhaps needed to be involved in their own right.

- **Funding.** The fact that local authorities were required to make a 30% contribution to MISG continued to be criticised, (Ivory, 1992). However, a greater number of funding sources were being used. One source was joint finance and in some areas the voluntary sector had been encouraged to find funding for themselves (Barnes 1994). This brought renewed calls for 100% grant finance, but it was also argued that local authorities should be forced to commit resources to MISG as it ensured that a political commitment was made by authorities to mental health over and above the community care budget (Brooker in GPMH/SSI, 1993; Barnes, 1994).

- **Who benefits?** Central to MISG projects is the care of people with 'severe mental illness' but, there was concern that the term was so broad, that the services funded by the grant were not always targeted to those most in need (Coia et al, 1994). One area of work which falls outside the remit of MISG, yet was valued highly by people providing services, was the raising of awareness of mental illness and preventative work (GPMH/SSI, 1993).

- **Recording**. Development of management information systems was needed for projects, and their parent organisation (DH/SSI, 1993b). In some cases it had become necessary to draw up a policy for handling information and confidentiality because of complex joint working arrangements.

SUMMARY OF THE POSITION IN 1993

4.24 It was clear in 1993 that MISG had enabled the development of a large range of different types of schemes, principally flexible, innovative and informal services operating with users taking a central position. New partnerships had grown up from effective joint work and variable experience of new contractual relationships had been gained. This had all been achieved while major changes in the organisation of health and social services had been implemented.

4.25 Research and monitoring showed that the grant had fulfilled many of its intentions but the question remained as to whether it had been able to do enough. Serious gaps in provision remained; very little attempt had been made to link MISG projects to CPA, and more work was required to ensure the effective involvement of users, carers and minority groups.

4.26 Also, strategic planning remained patchy. It was hampered by the limitations of needs assessment, which was, in turn, affected by the lack of availability of financial and management information. Within projects, it was identified that work was needed on the development of systematic monitoring, measurable quality standards and the provision of information for planning purposes.

4.27 Finally, the ring fencing of MISG resources was still considered to be crucial to maintain the momentum achieved. There was little sign of local authorities increasing their commitment to spending on mental health and care management funding was still too new to give confidence that the range of MISG projects could be assured continued financial support. For this reason, the temporary removal of uncertainty which resulted from the announcement in the 1994/5 MISG circular (*LAC(94)6*) that Ministers planned to extend MISG to 1997 was welcomed by all.

1994/5 AND BEYOND

4.28 The achievements and concerns about MISG were echoed in the announcement in February 1994 (*DH, 1994b*)—reaffirmed in February 1995—of the continuation of the grant. In the 1994 Circular reference is made to:

'the urgent need to build on this firm foundation by developing multi-disciplinary care planning and follow-up of mentally ill people by all relevant agencies.' (*LAC(94)6*)

It was again stressed that the grant was just one of a number of measures being taken to try to prevent mentally ill people slipping through the net of care. MISG projects were to continue to be innovative, and to reinforce good practice, but were to develop a focus on co-ordination between agencies, professions and individuals.

4.29 The 1995 Circular reinforces the call for better inter-agency co-operation in the planning and delivery of social care services for mentally ill people. It also requires local authorities to draw up a written Joint Strategy with local health authorities to ensure that resources and services are targeted on people with the most severe mental health problems. To support this development, the 1995 Circular confirmed that the grant would continue until at least 1997/98—subject to annual approval of funding by Parliament—and increased the level of the grant by £11.3 million, including £10 million of new money, to £47.3 million to support total expenditure of £66.6 million.

MISG ACTIVITY 1993/4

5

INTRODUCTION

5.1 This section of the report presents a brief summary of MISG activity in the financial year 1993/4. It gives a broad-brush picture of the number of MISG projects, the way they are managed, their type, purpose and main users. It also describes the expenditure involved. The information is derived from analysis of questionnaires sent to all local authorities in England as part of the Department of Health package inviting bids for MISG in 1994/5 (*see Appendix 1*).

Previous monitoring

5.2 Wherever relevant, reference is made to the findings of the two previous monitoring exercises which used similar questionnaires for data collection. However, comparisons are unsatisfactory for the following reasons:
- as the first monitoring was carried out in April 1991, it pre-dated MISG spending and examined proposed spend not actual spend
- monitoring of the actual use of MISG is available for the financial year 1991/2, (DH/SSI, 1993a) but the analysis was based on the ten old SSI regions which have subsequently been realigned into the four larger ones of South, North, Central and London.

For the purposes of this report, analysis has been based on the type of local authority. This enables a distinction to be made between activity in London, inner city areas and the shire counties. The main findings are set out below, and the more detailed tables are provided in Appendix 3.

Response rate

5.3 An overall response rate to the survey of just over 70% was achieved, but returns were uneven across the country and local authority type, as shown in Table 1. Thirty one replies were from county councils and only three from inner London.

Table 1 : Number of Local Authorities responding to survey

LA Type	No.	% of Returns	Number responding as % of all LA Type
Counties	31	44	78
Inner London	3	4	25
Outer London	11	15	55
Met Borough	26	37	72
	71	100	66

5.4 Approximately three quarters of counties and metropolitan boroughs responded, compared to half of outer London boroughs, and a quarter of inner London boroughs. In the second MISG monitoring exercise in

1991/2, a 100% response rate was achieved from authorities which received the grant.

NUMBER OF PROJECTS

5.5 The 71 authorities reported a total of 804 MISG funded projects currently in operation, or being set up. If this number was rounded up to take account of all LAs nationally, the total number of MISG projects in the country could be as high as 1,200. This compares very favourably with the results of the second monitoring which found in excess of 781 projects. However, both these figures could be regarded as underestimates. In 1992, returns concentrated on 'major' MISG developments, so excluding small MISG initiatives, and in 1994, some authorities only completed returns for new projects started during the year in question.

Table 2 : The Number of MISG Projects in LAs

LA Type	No. of LA	No. of Projects	% of Total Projects	Average No. of Projects per LA
Counties	31	565	70	18
Inner London	3	22	3	7
Outer London	11	70	8	8
Met Borough	26	147	18	8
	71	804	100	11

5.6 Nearly three quarters of MISG projects were reported from county councils (Table 2) and 18 percent from metropolitan boroughs. On average, there were 18 projects per county, and 7–8 in all other types of authority.

MANAGEMENT OF PROJECTS, 1993/4

5.7 A very mixed picture emerged concerning the agencies managing MISG projects. Less than half the projects (49%) were managed solely by SSDs (*Fig 1*). The voluntary sector was clearly a substantial provider managing 37 % of projects overall, and over 40% of MISG services in the metropolitan and inner London boroughs. The involvement of the private sector was negligible.

5.8 These findings demonstrate that there had been a small shift towards provision by the independent sector between 1991/2 and 1993/4. In 1991/2, the proportion of MISG projects run by SSDs was 53%, and 34% were run be independent agencies, while in 1993/4, 48% were SSD managed and 37% in the voluntary sector. This confirms that MISG appears to have contributed little to the development of the mixed economy of care, possibly because MISG increases since 1992/3 have been limited to inflation. Therefore, the pattern of MISG spending was largely set in the first year.

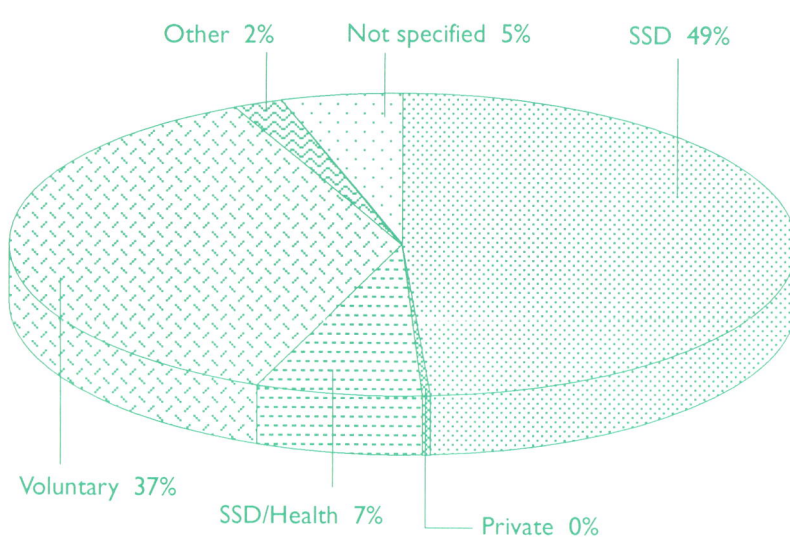

Figure 1: Management of MISG Projects

5.9 The findings also provided little evidence of projects being managed across agencies. Less than 10% of MISG schemes were jointly managed. The most common partnership was between health and social services (*57 projects*); only 14 projects were jointly managed by social services and a voluntary organisation. While this undoubtedly reflects the formal position, it does not identify many of the informal partnerships which have developed to enable independent organisations become new, effective providers of services (*see para 8.22*).

NEW PROJECTS OR EXTENSIONS OF EXISTING ONES

5.10 The objective of MISG is to enable SSDs to improve the social care of people with mental illness who need specialist psychiatric care but the improvement of care can come about from the extension of old services as well as the setting up of new ones. Unfortunately, the question in the survey on whether MISG projects were new or expanded services was often not satisfactorily completed and so the data collected is unreliable. However, it does suggest that half of the MISG projects operating in 1993/4 had been set up as new services while a third were expansions of older projects (*Table 3*).

Table 3: New or Existing Projects, 1993/4

LA Type	Extension of Existing	New Project
	% of Projects	% of Projects
Counties	38	50
Inner London	27	64
Outer London	26	64
Met Borough	40	42
% of Total	37	50
Total No.	295	403

Note: No information was provided on 13% of projects

5.11 Three hundred and fifty-two (44%) projects started in the first year of the grant, 1991/2 (*Fig 2*). In the second year, a further 30% became operational, partly because the grant increased by fifty percent, and partly because there was slippage of projects which were delayed in starting. The 1993/4 figures reflect the small annual growth in the grant, and the fact that most of the funding was committed to schemes already running.

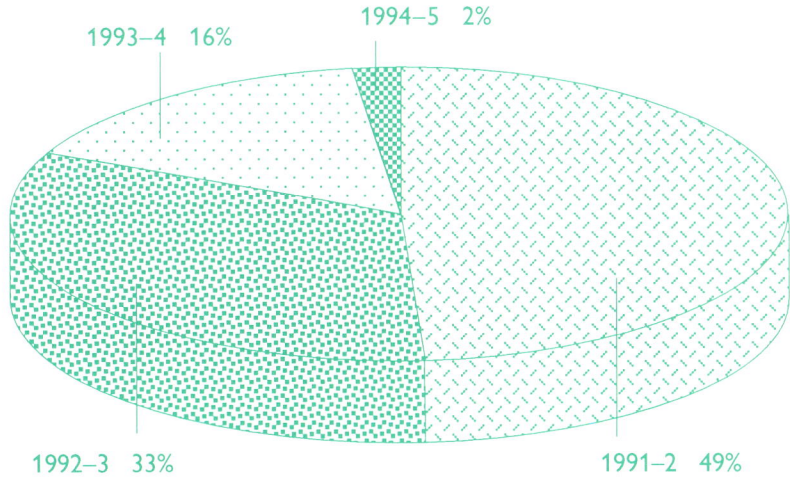

Figure 2: Start Date of Project

1994–5 2%
1993–4 16%
1992–3 33%
1991–2 49%

NATURE OF PROVISION

5.12 Table 4 shows the diversity of community care services provided by MISG. In order to obtain more detail of projects, further classification

MISG Activity 1993/4

of the main groups has been carried out. The methods used and the findings are explained in Appendix 3.

Table 4: Nature of Provision, 1993/4

Nature of Provision	No. of Projects	% of Total
Day care	202	25
Mental health team	171	21
Residential/housing	78	10
Employment	50	6
Drop-in	41	5
Carers	36	5
Home based service	35	4
Advocacy	34	4
Respite/relief care	23	3
Users' projects	22	3
Education/information	18	2
Befriending	17	2
Flexible/care management scheme	16	2
Training users	14	2
Training staff	13	2
Homeless	11	1
Leisure	9	1
Crisis intervention	9	1
MDO	5	0.6
Total	295	403

5.13 Almost half of the projects fell within the two umbrella categories of day services and mental health teams (MHT), and this dominant pattern was consistent throughout each type of local authority (see *Appendix 3*). Further analysis of these groups, together with the findings of the visits to local authorities, showed a trend away from building based services towards informal services offering individual help to people, often at home. This can be seen in the development of outreach services, specialist and support workers attached to mental health teams and in home based services (*Project Studies 3, 4, 8 and 10*).

5.14 MISG has not funded mental health teams as a whole, but has enabled specialist workers to join teams to:
- work with particular groups of users, such as people with long-term mental illness
- provide specific services such as skills training
- assist people to use education, leisure and social facilities in the community.

5.15 Residential /housing projects, and those targeted for the homeless, support a range of housing schemes, a mix of supported accommodation, development workers and care managers. Housing includes schemes for permanent accommodation, short stay, or staged housing and emergency beds. In all, 8 schemes were described as having an element of emergency accommodation or hospital avoidance (*Project Study 7*). Care management tended to be provided for the homeless.

5.16 Employment projects are of two types; those which prepare people for work and those which provide employment. Carers and respite schemes again emphasise the home based, and individual nature of services, but include some respite and carers' groups which run on different models (*Project Study 9*). The majority of the users' services are described as self-help projects (*Project Study 6*), but there are also groups which contribute to the planning process, and user-run services such as drop-ins.

5.17 An area of concern was that of mentally disordered offenders (MDO). It was hoped that MISG would be targeted specifically towards this client group as many community care plans highlight the need for such services, but there was no evidence of this development in 1993/4. However, it was clear that some of the MISG services offering support to people with mental illness include offenders amongst their users (*Para 5.21*).

OBJECTIVES

5.18 Local authorities were asked to identify the main objective of each of their MISG services in order to provide a general over-view of intention. The results are summarised in Figure 3, and more detailed information is provided in Appendix 3, Table A2. Some codes such as 'reducing hospital admission' have only been used when this is the specific objective of the project. It is assumed that most projects providing support in the community have this as their objective.

5.19 The main focus of MISG projects was to provide relief care and support to both service user and carers in the community. There were 136 projects which aimed to provide this and a further 117 projects offering support through:
- social and emotional support (*61 projects*)
- practical and domestic help (*42 projects*)
- networks (*14 projects*).

5.20 101 projects aimed to provide a safe but stimulating environment for users and 123 projects intended to enhance user choice or facilitate empowerment, including mutual support. The aim of 64 of the housing projects was to create accommodation opportunities and as many as 54 projects contributed to directly to the implementation of care management. Overall, only 29 projects provided services which were not directed specifically at service users and these included staff training, administrative support and the development of interagency networks.

Figure 3: The Objectives of MISG Projects

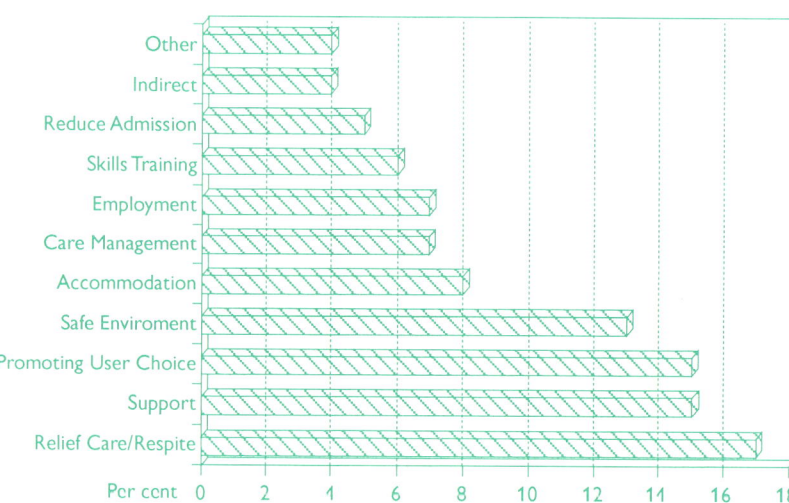

WHO ARE THE PROJECTS FOR?

5.21 In total, 62% of projects were targeted for people with severe mental illness under the age of sixty five and 36% for people over 65 (*Table 5*), but there was some overlap between these. In addition, many of these projects also targeted other priority groups. 51% of services were benefiting carers, 34% catered for people from black and minority ethnic communities and 31% provided for people resettling in the community after leaving long stay hospital. Despite the low number of projects set up for mentally disordered offenders, in all, 17% of projects welcome them. These projects are spread through all types of local authority (*see Appendix 3*).

5.22 Seventy-five projects were identified as projects for people with dementia. These included a wide range of types of services but 37% were day services and 31% provided relief care or support for carers. Over half of these services had relief care and support as their main objective.

5.23 From the information provided in the survey it was possible to identify 37 projects aimed specifically for people from minority ethnic communities: 15 for Asian people, 12 for Afro-Caribbean people, 8 for black and ethnic minority people generally and two for Jewish communities. Eleven projects provided day care, 8 advocacy and 7 specialist workers in mental health teams.

Table 5: Target Groups and Age Groups

Target Group	Under 65		Over 65	
	No of Projects	No of Service Users	No of Projects	No of Service Users
Severely MI in the community	500	31,125	282	19,371
Carers	240	6,207	169	8,266
Black and minority ethnic people	216	6,042	55	504
Resettled from long stay hospital	204	5,762	49	505
Homeless people	153	4,389	15	71
Mentally disordered offenders	134	1,052	1	5
Other groups	85	5,411	29	1,153

Note: i) Totals are not given in Table 5 as projects can target their services at more than one group. The total number of projects for which information was supplied is 804.

ii) Other groups include, under 25s, families, single parents, persons in crisis, older people in residential and nursing homes, people with learning disabilities and children of women with post natal depression.

NUMBER OF PEOPLE USING SERVICES

5.24 The number of people using MISG projects, indicated in Table 5 (*above*), has to be examined with caution as local authorities varied in the way that they interpreted this information. In some authorities, actual usage figures were entered, while in others, the potential number of beneficiaries were given. This was particularly problematic for services, such as information services, which could have a vast audience.

EXPENDITURE

5.25 Appendix 1 of the MISG Circular, LAC(94)6, contained questions about local authority spending on services for mentally ill people in the financial years 1992/3 and 1993/4, and the following section summarises the responses received. More detailed information is provided in Tables A7-A12 in Appendix 4. Eighty local authorities, including only 2 inner-London boroughs, responded to this part of the monitoring. This represents a 74% response rate, and it should be stressed that the information given below only refers to the responding authorities.

5.26 However, DH records show that 100% of MISG allocation for 1993/4 was taken up by 31st March 1994.

5.27 There was an 18% increase in overall expenditure by SSDs on services for mentally ill people from approximately £66.5 million in 1992/3 to approximately £78.5 million in 1993/4. It should be noted, however, that no correction has been made for inflation, and that 27% of the increase is attributable to the 70% contribution to MISG made by the

MISG Activity 1993/4

central government. Thus, 73% of the £12 million overall increase was provided from sources other than the central government's contribution to MISG, not allowing for inflation.

5.28 During the two financial years under study, around 75% MISG was spent on SSD managed schemes. Services managed by the voluntary and private sector accounted for some 20% of MISG expenditure.

5.29 From 1992/3 to 1993/4, the trends, though small, were away from solely SSD managed projects (*76% down to 71%*) and towards voluntary and private sector managed services (*18% up to 23%*). The percentage of joint health/SSD managed projects remained roughly the same at about 4.5% to 5%.

5.30 No information was received about the sources of local authority expenditure on services for the mentally ill unrelated to MISG. Possible 'other' sources are the SSD base budget and joint health/SSD funding.

5.31 Approximately four-fifths of authorities found the 30% local contribution towards MISG from base budget with most of the rest coming from joint finance. This pattern was consistent over the two years of study although the amount raised from 'other' sources increased slightly in 1993/4.

THE VIEWS OF MISG SERVICE USERS

6

A principle aim of the this monitoring exercise was to examine the views of the people using MISG projects. In this section, the aspects of MISG services most valued by users are identified but further comment and criticism from users can be found in Sections 7 and 8.

SUPPORT AND UNDERSTANDING

Support

"I have a social worker and if I am poorly I will talk with him but the lasses here are very good. I've been poorly on a couple of occasions and they have even come up to the house. I need a good telling off sometimes when I am naughty. You can go and see a psychiatrist and he gives you pills. Other than that, I think they are useless. I can't honestly say they have done me a lot of good because they haven't, and I must have had just about every pill that is out, you know."

"They are very supportive. They leave it you to you whether to take ideas up or not. They are moving me on but I do the work."

"I need the company but I am doing much more on my own now with someone here to help."

"I get very depressed and I like the group. I enjoy it and we get on well together. Its helped me a lot or else I don't think I would still be here like this—I would be in a nut house or something."

"I used to go to the day hospital and I heard about this place. They are worth their weight in gold, these lasses. I just couldn't cope with life—I was in and out of hospital—but once I was down here, I know I have got support."

Mutual support

"The people who come can support and encourage each other."

"It makes a big difference going out together. We know all what we like, and we know our capabilities."

"I like people, and I always have done, so I like coming on the bus. We are all in the same boat and you can talk about it. If you can talk about it happily, you can help one another."

"They don't care for you at the hospital once you are away. We care—we can ring each other up. I don't sleep well and I don't mind picking up the phone at night if someone is down. It would be nice to link up with one of us rather than a CPN. There isn't any help they can give apart from medication, and putting you in hospital—there just isn't any."

Understanding

"Everyone is wonderful. I am not long out of hospital and everyone is marvellous. They understand I get these turns."

The Views of MISG Service Users

"Understanding each other is one of the main things. People might just bump into you, and, even if they have known you a long time, they don't know what you are going through."

"Unless you really understand the condition people get into who suffer mental illness, you won't really know what people go through. Its not nice. Its not pleasant at all. I'm better now and this is a stepping stone. Its given me time to adjust. Its given me stability in between when I came here, and when I get sorted out the other end with a flat."

"You don't have anyone else you can talk to. Even if you have a family they don't want to know you and they can't understand you."

"You can talk to the family but it is difficult to explain how you feel yourself. Here people understand. Most of us are going through similar problems so we understand."

"The people make the place special. A lot are isolated by mental illness. If I am talking to someone and I go a blank, people think you are an utter fool. You are just trying to think and it doesn't come out. You relax here. It doesn't matter that you stumble or can't speak. We just laugh. The understanding is the basic thing."

Information

"I gave up my job when he came out of hospital. They wanted to put him in a home but I didn't want it, and I knew he wouldn't want it. I am in all the time with him. I get satisfaction from it but it isn't easy. It helps to come here, to talk and learn. I came to see what I could learn and I have been coming here ever since." (**Carer**)

FRIENDSHIP

Friendship

"All the people here have something wrong with their nerves so they can all relate to one another. When I was really depressed, I was just going to bed and shutting the door. I had a drink problem as well but, fortunately, I have been able to get over that. To me its a place to come where everybody is friendly—we have trips and holidays. There is not much we don't do. Its gets you out and about, and stops you moping in the house. In fact I would say its a life saver for me. I am sure if my husband were here he would agree with me. He likes me to come. He knows where I am and he is not worried all day. I am with friends."

"You get to know each other quite well. We are like brothers and sisters. Its lovely."

"Its a right nice crowd of people. If anybody does you a good turn, its from kindness. Its a lovely club."

Company

"It gives you company through the day."

"Seeing somebody you know—I can't get out much."

"I come for the company as much as anything. You've got people to help if you have got worries about anything. For those of us who live on our own, its nice to come here and have someone to talk to."

"You mix with different people and get interested in different people."

New faces

"I haven't any friends but the wife, so its new faces."

Removes loneliness

"It takes away a little bit of the loneliness. My kids are in America so I have no-one."

"I am lonely at home all the time. There is nobody to talk to."

"I have my own sister and mother and everybody but it is still lonely."

"I get very angry. I just scream. I am not always smiling. I get lonely."

"I just like being with the other women. I don't need to talk -its just being here."

Everybody gets on

"It is special because it is somewhere to come when you feel so lonely and they are most understanding people. We all get on fine together. We never have any trouble. Everybody is kind and, if anybody is poorly, we collect and send them flowers to cheer them up."

"You feel its somewhere you can go—its a bit like having a big family"

"I like to come 2 days a week. I want to be here all the time because they are very kind and caring. Here I feel I am wanted. We are all a big family. We look after each other. On trips the happiness is great. People are mad if they don't like it here."

GETTING OUT

Looking forward

"You get relaxed from coming here. You can talk about whatever you like to the group. Once you go home, its finished so you can look forward to cooking or whatever. It helps. I am looking forward to Tuesdays all the time."

"We can say, 'Oh my God, the weekend is so hopeless', but then Monday comes and you are OK. This morning I was so relaxed, I was coming out and not looking at nothing."

"I went to Tenerife. I had never been on a plane before—when the door opened and it was all that sunshine oh.......... I couldn't get over it. It was snowing at home. All being well in 1996 we might be going back. I am looking forward to it already."

The Views of MISG Service Users

Getting out

"It has given me something to look forward to during the week."

"Its something to look forward to. I get ready on Wednesday night for Thursday morning."

"I feel as though I have to come. Its a very good thing. It gets me out the house."

"Its good to have somewhere to go."

"You find yourself trapped at home. I've had plenty of the four walls."

"People talking, game of bingo, raffles, friendship—you get away from yourself being with people and if you have been stuck in the house, you are getting away from your own environment. I felt really off it this morning. I feel better now. Sometimes they will ring to see if you are all right."

"Its something to look forward to knowing you will go out. Over the weekend I don't go out. I used to go out every day when I could walk."

"Its very nice. It makes a change. I don't get out much as I can't drive now. I used to have a three-wheeler. Where I live there is only a bus on a Wednesday and a Friday."

"Life would be impossible without these trips."

"I feel I must keep going when I can. I look well but I feel like a robot sometimes. The tablets wear you out."

SHARING MEALS AND CELEBRATIONS

Meals

"For some people its not a great deal like but, if you have been stuck in the house, its a godsend. You can come down here if you have got nobody at home, you get a damn good meal, some one to talk to."

Celebrations

"We try to put birthdays together and celebrate them."

"I can remember a few bleary eyes last Christmas. It was very good, very friendly—you are all together. We are not too big a group to go out together—we get into groups of 4 and change around."

TALKING

Talking

"The chance to talk—we talk about everything."

"Being able to talk in private."

"There's certain things I can talk to P about because I suffer with depression."

WORKERS

Workers

"You need someone to take responsibility. Everyone has had problems obviously or we wouldn't be here. We have all been ill people and there are still a lot of ill people here. You just couldn't get a group together week after week without someone being in charge."

"The worker helps us fit in. We have never had any trouble in the group but its nice having them."

"I like having a support worker who doesn't have to go by the book. I have had therapy enough. Its nice to get with someone who doesn't want to know all about you. I can just tell her things if I want to."

Confidentiality

"The most important thing is the freedom to talk, knowing it is confidential, knowing people will listen, being with people."

"It makes you feel relaxed. If it wasn't for this place I don't know what I would do. I used to take a lot of overdoses and since I come here .... They are just great—they make you feel at home, and they make you feel welcome and you can talk to them and what you say won't go no further. They really look after you. They give you advice."

OTHER

Confidence

"It gives me confidence."

"Gives me a chance to stand on my own."

"Its the saving grace. It has helped."

"I was quite pleased with my goal planning—it made me realise I had done more than I thought."

"On some occasions it has stopped me thinking about suicide. So I am quite happy to be here, and be a survivor."

Gender

"You still need the woman's thing; it is very difficult to change. We can relate to women better. It is essential that these women can be separate."

"Personally, I prefer a male worker."

"There is a lack of men staff and only one male volunteer."

The Views of MISG Service Users

No stigma

"The difficulty is ignorance. People who look different are not treated right in the community. Here you are treated as an individual and an equal."

"People who know you and know you have been in hospital will bring it up. They don't let you live it down. You don't feel like that here. We are all different in our feelings but we understand.

ASPECTS OF GOOD PRACTICE

7

7.1 The SSI team found that MISG was supporting many exciting new and innovative projects which would have been unlikely to develop without the grant. Both from the work carried out by the team, and from the comments of service users, some key aspects of good practice were identified and are described in the following section.

Responsive

7.2 Projects recognised the need for flexibility in order to respond effectively to:
- the individual needs of users and carers
- changes in these need
- the call for help at any time of the night or day.

> **RESPONSIVE TO THE NEEDS OF CLIENTS**
>
> *"I like any flexibility and freedom we have of choice so we can keep our individuality and not be labelled. It is important to be able to have change without fear of retaliation."*
>
> Firstly, clients appreciate knowing the support they receive can be stepped up, or down, depending on how well they are.
>
> *"When I am bad they come a few times a week."*
> *"I am going to need more help soon. My worker has foreseen it. It helps to know they are there. It helps me to face what is coming."*
>
> Secondly, clients appreciated being able to change their support worker after a time because workers, and clients, need change.
>
> *"Its not nice to be tied to one individual or even two. If you were making your own mates you would choose them."*
> *"You can change worker, I found that out and they don't take it funny either. Its not so much changing as interchanging."*
>
> Thirdly, clients like the freedom to talk or not to talk.
>
> *"I don't necessarily delve deeply but I did a few months ago and its nice to know I can."*

"I would like to see a Support Worker at weekends. Some weekends you feel so lousy, you need someone to talk to. Sometimes talking on the phone is like talking to the bottle of tablets that you are going to take at the end of the day."

Aspects of Good Practice

24 HOURS A DAY

The team is accessible to clients on a 24 hour basis.

"I can phone the Rehab Team in the evening. Just having someone to talk to is all you need sometimes. It saves you getting the doctor out. You chat on the phone, put the phone down and you've eased your conscience. You have talked your problem out. You have talked when perhaps you were suicidal. You feel warmer—better—you go to bed and go to sleep."

Occasionally sleep-ins are needed and a community support worker will stay with a client overnight. Care is taken not to let the service be abused:

"I would rather see a support worker relieve a tired carer than stay with someone who would be better off in hospital."(**Manager**)

Although the team does not run a blue light service, they do respond to emergencies, and are called out by the Emergency Duty Team and the police if one of their clients is having problems. Through knowing the client and their illness, the team can calm situations and ensure appropriate response is given. They can prevent unnecessary hospital admissions, or, if admission is required, help to persuade the client to go in voluntarily.

"J knows how to calm my wife down now. She is getting to know her and she got her into hospital quietly the other evening. It important to act here before the neighbours do."

Miss Armstrong is very forgetful, not remembering the day of the week, or the time of the day, and so she tends to forget to eat. She receives considerable input from a variety of services; Home Care seeing to her breakfast and tea, and the Companion Service to her lunch. Despite her forgetfulness, she is very particular in her habits and won't be hurried. As a result, the home care worker often has to move on to the next client before Miss Armstrong has finished her meal and so the mess is left in the kitchen. The companion, by allowing an extra half hour for her visit, invariably sorts out the mess while Miss Armstrong takes her time getting herself settled for the afternoon.

> **READY ACCESS**
>
> In addition to running the day club, the workers maintain an informal telephone help line to support members when the club is closed. In their experience, the line is rarely abused because members understand their need for time with their families. The workers do not go out in response to a call, but they give advice, and get appropriate help.
>
> *"I find the wife's problems start on a Friday. You cannot get a doctor or anybody like that—any help—and you are stuck until Monday morning. You just don't know what is going to happen. Like when there is someone on call over the weekend you can get a bit of guidance. Cath and Sally will get in touch with the doctor if they can't help—we get good support now—its lovely. Its been a boon."* (**Carer**)

Culturally sensitive

7.3 Many MISG projects were sensitive to the needs of people from minority ethnic communities and some separate projects have been developed. They have created an environment where people from ethnic communities can feel relaxed, and where they can get appropriate support and understanding in their own language. The experience of users of these projects was that existing mental health services often provided none of these things.

"The services that are provided are not catering for the ethnic community. There are services like Breast Cancer Support and Diabetic Support but ethnic people don't have the confidence to use these services because they are set up and run predominantly by non-ethnic people. What somebody would have to do is set up an ethnic support group. This building we are in is the mental health day centre. Our users can't use it during the day—there are men here, people are smoking, there are different activities that are not culture specific. You have to listen to music that is not culturally ours. You want to do your own things. The services that do exist just aren't appropriate." (**Worker**)

"I am more angry than anything now because of what I did—what I ended up doing, and what I have become—because there isn't anything out there. There isn't any other help...... Its like shouting and saying to someone, 'For God sake do something'."

"Our culture is very important. I think a lot of my culture and I don't want people to tell me that in 2 years time you will meet someone else because I am never going to meet someone—that's not in my culture. I don't want to meet somebody. My husband was my first and my only." (**Widow**)

Aspects of Good Practice

Keeping an eye out

7.4 Projects have placed importance on their role in monitoring the health and well being of users. The workers watch for changes and take action when necessary. They may be able to respond appropriately themselves, or they may need to seek the involvement of others. Some projects have developed agreements with users as to when workers can intervene on their behalf, and what information can be shared.

"If you can nip it in the bud, you can stop a crisis. We can open doors by picking up the phone and getting help." (**Worker**)

"In hospital it is very frightening—I spent 3 months there and I saw some funny things. I am worried about people coming out of hospital. At least this place keeps people on an even keel and it is less worrying."

"When I come in and Sally says, 'Hello', her eyes light up and I feel good. The workers look at me and see that I am tidy—they tell how I feel that way."

> **SUPPORTING OLDER PEOPLE**
>
> Although the project appears to be easy going, happy and casual, it has had to be professional in its approach and in the delivery of the service. Often the project is the only service people have; they are referred by social workers or community nurses and their case is closed. Therefore, the workers are responsible for monitoring client's well being and reacting appropriately if there is cause for concern.

Working with risk

7.5 The assessment, and acceptance, of risk was a necessary part of the work of many MISG projects which support very vulnerable people in the community. Workers were dealing with situations where users could be a risk to themselves or to others. Workers also often found themselves contributing to decisions about the need for admission to hospital or, in the case of older people, the need for admission to nursing or residential care homes.

> **MINIMISING RISK**
>
> The Support Team often finds itself alone with clients who will not accept help. If someone is not ill enough to be compulsorily admitted to hospital under the Mental Health Act, but is going down and refusing treatment, there may be little workers can do except be there two or three times a day every day and make sure all the appropriate people know where help can be reached quickly.
>
> *"Colleagues know, and the police know, that we just have to try to be there before things blow up. Sometimes we have to let people breakdown to get them into hospital."* **(Worker)**

> **THE RISK OF LIVING ALONE WITH DEMENTIA**
>
> *" You feel a lot are a bit unsafe, but a lot are capable of being on their own. They need a little bit of support, particularly if they haven't any family near."* (Companion)
>
> *"They feel so much better in the community. They stay so much more alert too. For them its nice that they can stay in the home which they have lived in for years."* (Companion)
>
> *"We have maintained people who would have gone in sooner. We have given people, and their families, time to decide. Some have made the decision that they want to go in and be looked after but, for some, it hasn't been easy. The family realises that there is no choice when their relative no longer knows the Companion, or the room they are sitting in. They get distressed by the change and we continue visiting for a month. Some die within a week. There often isn't a right time—you would need a crystal ball."*
> **(Director)**

Interagency working

7.6 Projects did not work in isolation but demonstrated their commitment to providing a service within a local network of care through their work with other mental health agencies. This took a variety of forms:
- referral to other professions and agencies for help with individual users, for example, through CPA and care management structures
- sharing records with other agencies who share the care of someone who is confused

> **CONTINUOUS CARE RECORD**
>
> To help communication between different workers, a Continuous Care Record is sometimes kept which is completed by each care worker who goes into the house. This is particularly helpful where complex care arrangements are in place such as those for Miss Armstrong. She has home care morning and tea time, a companion at lunch time, a private cleaner, regular visits from the nurse and doctor and support from her two nieces. She likes to see her care record and will remind workers to write on it if it catches her eye. In other homes the record is kept out of reach so that it doesn't go missing.
>
> *"M's care record is written in a book and, as she like to read it when she is alone at night, we will write messages and stories for her".* (**Worker**)

- ensuring professionals are familiar with projects, for example by inviting CPNs and social workers to visit the project informally or to take part in activities. Also, home based project workers encourage their clients to use services being run by other agencies in their locality such as day centres or clubs.
- ensuring interagency contact and advice from skilled and experienced professionals/ managers through project steering groups made up of staff from social services, health, user organisations and other relevant organisations.

> **STEERING COMMITTEE**
>
> Members of the police, health and social services support the club through a Steering Committee which is particularly helpful in maintaining interagency understanding and the exchange of information. Two members of the club also attend the Steering Group and feed back information to the club.

- avoidance of duplication in service provision; for example, workers knowing the boundaries of what the projects provides or sharing opening on a Saturday and Sundays.

"You might start off visiting 2 days a week and build up to daily visits. When you start getting people up and dressed that's not our job and so Home Care comes in." (**Worker**)

User Involvement

7.7 Projects have encouraged users to participate in the running of the service and to assert choice. This sometimes took the form of canvassing users' opinions and gaining feedback from them.

> **HEARING FROM USERS OF A HOME BASED SERVICE**
>
> Clients are encouraged to participate in deciding the direction of the service, and, as it is a home-based service, ad hoc meetings are held to which all clients are invited. These attract a small but active attendance and generate some very useful information. At the first meeting, clients explained that they would prefer to receive questionnaires to canvass their opinion than have to speak out at a meeting and so this has been put into practice. When a topic is to be discussed, for example flexible hours, a questionnaire is sent out and a meeting called to discuss the results.

In projects where interaction was possible, user committees had been set up. These varied from being structured and unstructured, facilitated and unfacilitated, directed by staff or controlled by users. In most of the projects, the process of involvement in the group was as important as what the group achieved.

> **A MISG PROJECT RUN BY USERS**
>
> Members are very careful to enable each other to participate in the running of the group. Monthly business meetings are held to share this task and although meetings are informal, a chairperson and secretary have been appointed.
>
> *"I just make sure that everything is discussed and stop people talking when someone else is."* (**Chair**)
>
> *"I take down the notes so we know everything that's happened. Its good because we tend to forget. At the next meeting we can go over what's happened and see if there are notes of what is to be discussed this time."* (**Secretary**)
>
> The notes of meetings are typed up and circulated to all members so that they can all be kept informed of what's going on and keep a record. The benefit of the record is that:
>
> *"It keeps your mind going to think about the group and to plan."*

"We have a members committee which meets every month to make plans. Once a year we are asked if we would like to stand for the committee and we vote to elect six members. Meetings are very informal—we don't write things down—we just check things out at the end with the workers."
(**Committee Member**)

Aspects of Good Practice

> **COMMUNITY AND ADVOCACY MEETINGS**
>
> All members are welcome at the Community Meeting which is informal and run by the workers. Members feel it gives them a say in what is going on.
>
> *"It tells us what's going on. It is both ways. It is very helpful. Everybody has a say here. You have to be reasonable about it."*
>
> *"We had an Advocacy Meeting as well. That was where we had everybody in the big hall, who are members or whatever, and it got a chance for them to express how they feel, how they were treated and things about their accommodation or whatever. This did not always feed into the Community meeting, but people could do it if they wanted. They could come in if they want and say whatever they wished to say. There was always free speech."*

Carers and families

7.8 Many services which were not targeted specifically for carers did extend their activities to include families and friends. This was not general practice as some projects stressed the importance of providing a service exclusively for users but, in other services, the involvement of families was welcomed. Examples of shared involvement which suited the particular projects concerned were:

- sharing information and care with the family.

"We are like the family. We are not official like the doctors and social workers—we are on the same level as the family so they can talk to us more. You build up a friendship with the family." (**Worker**)

- involving families in activities with the agreement of the users.

"Its very sociable. I come and help out occasionally—my mum comes every day. She lives to come here. She thinks the world of the workers—nothing is too much trouble—they help her, and even the family. A lot of people don't know what the family is going through when people are poorly. You can talk to Cath and Sally. They encourage families to come. They are very caring." (**Daughter**)

- including families on outings and holidays.

"I am a carer. For me its smashing. Up to two year ago we hadn't been away. We hadn't had a holiday for 14 years. The wife come here and they run holidays from here. I went with them and I felt secure like I had an insurance policy. We went away with their help and support. It was a real holiday break. Hopefully we will go again next year." (**Carer**)

- adjusting to both the needs of users and their carers.

"Our group is for carers but some sufferers will come. Often carers won't leave them. I can get a sitting service in if they would like to come alone but they don't—we are like one big family." (**Organiser**)

> **USERS' NEEDS, CARERS' NEEDS**
>
> The flexibility of the Activity Bus was demonstrated by the support given to a woman with very poor mobility. She was offered a weekly trip on the bus but, as she didn't want to leave her house, the bus dropped off a volunteer to sit with her and took her carer on the trip instead. This way her carer got out, had a break and was able to do her shopping in town while the other passengers had coffee.

- recognising the needs of carers after the person they are caring for has had to be admitted to a care home or has died.

"They have lost the person they were caring for and the trauma of that loss has left them so empty after the years of doing the same thing. Nobody says, 'There's a life out there', while you are caring, so they have lost everything. For some people Alzheimer's Disease becomes their life." (**Organiser**)

Transport

7.9 The provision of transport to enable projects to be used was essential for some services. The circumstances where this was necessary were:
- rural areas with very poor public transport
- groups for people with mobility problems who needed specially adapted transport
- groups for people with very low motivation who had difficulty getting out
- services for people from minority ethnic communities who felt unsafe or uneasy on public transport.

Information

7.10 Good information was a priority for users, planners and providers of services but it was not often available.

> **MAROONED**
>
> MAROONED? is a mental health newsletter which keeps clients of the Support Team in touch with what's going on. It has developed from a dull looking pamphlet into a bright looking newsletter and has input from clients, staff and people interested and active in mental health. It has a fast growing circulation, being distributed to 150 clients and ex-clients of the Support Team by the workers, and to an increasing number of professionals, services and voluntary sector agencies. 450 copies are produced but, with this number, stocks run out in a matter of weeks and so production is going to have to expand again.
>
> Success has been judged not just on the growth of demand but from its popularity with survivors. The editor now feels that he has got to know what people want and has no difficulty in getting material to print.
>
> *"Its just important to write in a friendly style with stories from support workers and others who the clients will know. The main difficulty is that I have got too much material. There is a danger that if you put too much in it and it could become daunting."*
> **(Editor)**

Support and supervision

7.11 Projects with robust arrangements for staff support and supervision were to be commended. Support is especially important for staff working in isolated situations in the community. This can be difficult, and expensive, to provide on a 24 hour basis but one solution adopted by some home based projects is to work from a day centre or residential establishment at the weekend where support is available. All care staff, and most particularly those who are unqualified, should have regular supervision from a professional or experienced worker.

> **SUPERVISION FOR THE TEAM**
>
> Mutual support is provided within the team but there is also a well planned system for staff supervision, support and safety. The Team Leader is supervised by the manager and, in turn, supervises the Rehabilitation Officers(RO). The ROs supervise the Community Support Workers (CSW). Overall case responsibility is held by the social worker/care manager and the ROs meet the social workers on a weekly basis.

Safety

7.12 Considerable attention had been paid to staff safety in some projects in which workers could be placed in situations of risk. Most common was a policy of visiting potentially dangerous users in pairs and setting up effective back-up systems.

> **STAFF SAFETY**
>
> On sleep-ins, CSWs have the mobile phone and a bleep so that staff can contact them. An RO, or the Team Leader, always remains on call. Similar back-up is available in emergencies. ROs respond to threatened overdoses, but if the situation is found by a CSW, he/she will bleep the RO. They will call the GP and/or ambulance and involve the Psychiatric Centre as appropriate. If the client has to go to casualty, an ambulance will be called as staff can not take clients who are threatening self-harm in their own cars for their own, and the client's, safety. When facing aggressive or violent situations, the Approved Social Worker on duty is called. If staff are in any doubt at all about their safety, they must visit in pairs.

Teamwork

7.13 Teamwork was acknowledged as particularly important in projects where:
- working staff visit each others clients during evenings and weekends;
- user's dependency on a particular worker needs to be avoided;
- workers visit together when exposed to potentially dangerous situations;
- workers valued each other's different abilities and skills so apportioning work with clients to the worker with the most appropriate skills.

Training

7.14 As many MISG projects were dependent on unqualified workers, and they are pioneering new approaches to the delivery of care to people living in the community, considerable emphasis was placed on training.

> **INITIAL TRAINING FOR WORKERS**
>
> To ensure the support workers are appropriately, and adequately, trained, a training course was devised which gave workers a City and Guilds qualification in developing a mental health service. This included aspects such as the philosophy of care, mental illness, resources and structures. In addition to being successful in training the new team, the course had spin-offs such as team building and establishing the basis of the mental health resource data base.

Aspects of Good Practice

PLANNING AND MANAGEMENT ISSUES

8

FINANCIAL PLANNING

MISG

8.1 The significance of MISG for SSDs was not so much the size of the grant, but the fact it was mental health money, ring fenced for mental health services, available at a time of widespread economic difficulty and fundamental change. The allocation to each authority made up only a small part of departmental spend on mental health, and yet officers described 'heavy dependence' on it to fund services and to raise the political profile of mental health.

Mental Health Spend

8.2 Overall social services expenditure on mental health remains low. In the authorities visited, only two spent in excess of 5% of their SSD budget on mental health and one authority spent less than 3%. However, this expenditure was widely acknowledged to be unacceptably low and the trend was upward. SSDs were finding a variety of ways achieving this:
- increasing the proportion of base budget allocated to mental health
- targeting joint finance—this was particularly used to redress an imbalance of resources between health authorities within a county
- greater use of STG for mental health services; some authorities had a policy of targeting a different user group each year and others specifying the proportion to be spent on mental health annually
- putting pressure on health purchasers to transfer savings from hospital retraction into community services.

Spending

8.3 Authorities were able to spend their grant allocation within the year. The annual uplift in the grant introduced in April 1993 provided few opportunities for growth as it was only a little above inflation. The majority of authorities visited had tried to compensate for this by bidding, with variable success, for a share of grant monies which became available late in the financial year. In general, they would have welcomed a larger allocation of the grant.

8.4 On the other hand, the small annual increase minimised the difficulties some authorities faced in finding the 30% contribution. Hardest hit were authorities which had been subject to capping measures, but a range of solutions were found, often using combinations of SSD base budget, STG, joint finance and the allocation of in-house provision such as home care for mental health users.

8.5 In some authorities, MISG had a 'snowball' effect, attracting other financial support to projects and related services. Also, some projects were able to increase their resources through spot contracting—using STG—so enabling them to expand in response to identified local need.

Financial Issues

8.6 The following issues concerning finance were found during the study:
- the continuing low levels of spending on mental health by SSDs

- the lack of financial information available from SSDs on mental health expenditure in general and on accounting for MISG in particular
- the small annual increase provided in 1993/4 which limited the development potential of the grant and therefore restricted its strategic value. The small increase reduced the possibilities for innovation. In addition, some projects were victims of their own success, running into overspend because of high take up which MISG funding was unable to keep pace with.
- widespread misunderstanding of the future of MISG finance if, and when, the specific grant ends. The end of the grant might mean an end to the ring fencing placed around the MISG finance already allocated but not an end to existing money itself. This would continue to be paid to local authorities and would be taken into the Standard Spending Assessment allocations. Therefore, whether or not the money remains invested in the mental health services which have set up by MISG would be a decision for local politicians.
- the time limited nature of the specific grant which created uncertainty in authorities where there was a lack of political commitment to continue funding projects if MISG ring fencing were to be withdrawn. Typically, in such projects, the staff were on short-term contracts, users felt insecure and the whole service felt undervalued.

"It gets me the funding. We have to go out with tins on pub crawls. We have done this but Probation doesn't have to. Are we the poor relations of Probation?" (**MIND Day Centre**)

STRATEGIC PLANNING

Mental Health Strategy

8.7 Authorities with an agreed mental health strategy were able to take the opportunity presented by MISG to progress the strategy in the absence of other growth monies. MISG was even described by one authority as 'seeding' a cultural change by stimulating the development of new services which responded to the expressed needs of users. However, these authorities were found to be the exception rather than the rule. The level of strategic planning for mental health continued to be underdeveloped. Strategies tended to be statements of general direction and lacked specificity on goals, measurable outcomes, time scales and responsibilities.

Deterrents

8.8 The following deterrents to the adoption of a strategic approach to mental health development were identified:
- the lack of a financial foundation for a strategy. This discouraged the investment of time and energy in the development of a strategy. One authority had built in provisos that the strategy was unlikely to be operationalised in full because of the lack of resources. Another authority refused to move into strategic planning and away from what was 'realistic', or had committed funding.
- difficulties in ensuring adequate participation of the many stakeholders in the planning process. Where widespread

involvement was achieved, the process tended to be prolonged, and care was needed to avoid creating complex strategies which needed a great deal of further work to operationalise.
- under-development of the assessment of mental health need in the community. Few authorities had invested in either internal or external research upon which a strategy could be based.
- difficulties over working strategically with health authorities and health providers. Examples of these were:
  - the re-configuration of health authority boundaries. For example, in one authority, the number of health authorities had reduced from 5 to 3 and then to 2
  - patchy planning over some county areas because of the differing attitudes of individual health authorities
  - health authorities and social services continuing to have different priorities concerning mental health investment
  - the lack of health providers on planning groups in health authorities where the purchasers had very little knowledge of mental health services
  - the recent introduction of joint health commissioning which had again altered the planning process and staff involved.

Strategic Issues

8.9 The principle strategic concerns were:
- the grant helped to force the pace of joint planning by requiring decisions on MISG spend to be taken jointly by health and social services but this was often done independently of strategic planning
- explanations of the use of MISG in Community Care Plans (as required by the NHS and Community Care Act 1990, Section 46) were sparse, with some authorities providing no information at all about MISG
- the value of MISG for pump-priming and experimentation was recognised but development tended to be incremental rather than strategic
- projects tended to stem from good ideas; they were not planned or linked to developments.

EXAMPLE OF GOOD PRACTICE IN BIDDING FOR MISG

As part of the internal bidding process for MISG in one authority, applicants for the grant were required to illustrate:

- how the project fell within the framework of the published departmental objectives
- what links existed with CPA
- how the project met the objectives of the joint mental health strategy
- what measures were in place to enable user and carer involvement in service development.

OPERATIONAL PLANNING

Implementation

8.10 Despite the widespread lack of strategic planning associated with MISG spending, some authorities were to be commended for highlighting the opportunities offered by MISG, publicising its availability, and rules, and inviting a wide range of organisations to bid for its funding. This approach helped to encourage innovative thinking and emphasise the opportunity to develop new services to reach hitherto unmet needs. Giving MISG a strong identity also helped in a few authorities to raise the political profile of mental health provision generally and the grant specifically.

EXAMPLE OF A FRAMEWORK FOR IMPLEMENTATION

In order to develop a systematic and consistent approach to facilitate the most effective use of MISG through 17 area offices, the SSD introduced a number of measures at an early stage:

- Each District identified an Area Manager to act as a Lead Manager for Mental Health.
- Departmental guidelines were produced to focus and limit the range of projects.
- There was early political commitment to finding the 30% contribution.
- The rules which applied to the grant were clarified and publicised.
- SSD's lead role was identified.
- A locally based, bottom-up planning approach was used.
- Distribution across the county recognised the previous resource inequities.
- The role of the voluntary sector was emphasised.
- There was a focus on non-capital dependent schemes.
- Care management was promoted with budgets allocated to buy services such as respite or day care.
- Training was included in each bid, including training for the private and voluntary sectors.
- Politicians agreed to the Director having delegated decision making to make adjustments to projects within the year.

Development

8.11 Three broad approaches were found in the ways in which MISG was invested in the authorities visited.
- A flagship project. Some authorities concentrated MISG investment in one main service which acted as the focus for a series of smaller projects. These flagship projects were invariably within the statutory sector whereas smaller projects tended to be a mix of

statutory and voluntary sector provision. In some cases the smaller projects were satellites of the main service (Project Studies 4 and 6).

> **EXAMPLE OF A FLAGSHIP PROJECTS-COMMUNITY SUPPORT WORKER SERVICE**
>
> This project has been set up to assist people with severe and enduring mental health problems within a framework of an integrated community mental health service. It helps to provide a wide range of therapeutic services, practical support, advice and advocacy as well as a large self-help network. The community support workers operate a flexible 7 days a week service and their activities include a rapid response to people assessed to be in immediate risk of hospitalisation, or other institutional care, by providing intensive support. Underpinning their work is a strong commitment to the Care Programme Approach.

- A mix of large and small projects with no particular connection between them. The small projects were often single workers such as family support workers, development workers and advocacy workers.

- An even distribution of smaller projects. Counties where decision making was devolved to districts, and where boundaries cover a number of health authorities, tended to have small projects distributed throughout their districts, each district having its share of the grant to spend. Formulae were applied in some cases to ensure equitable distribution of MISG.

8.12 Within the diverse range of projects developed with MISG, services were found to be in line with the criteria laid down for the grant. The largest area of growth has been the development of hands-on services provided by non-mental health professionals. The most notable characteristic of these services was the high motivation of staff and their encouraging results (Project Studies 3, 4 and 8).

8.13 MISG has also been involved in projects which cross client groups, but maintain a particular focus on people with mental health problems. Examples of these included interpretation services and development workers who were setting up support for young carers, as well as families and older people. None of this development would have been possible without the grant.

Operational Issues

8.14 The lack of experience many authorities had had of developing community services gave rise to concern. Even where there was a clear vision of what services were needed, due consideration was not always given to who, or what agency, would be best to develop and provide the service. Because decisions tended to be opportunistic, commercial viability and potential for expansion were ignored. Judging from the changes which have occured in the role of some MISG projects since they were set up two or three years ago, attention also needed to be given to identifying more clearly at the outset exactly what was required.

8.15 At project level, there was sometimes a disturbing lack of awareness of MISG with little understanding of its rules and intentions. For some projects, MISG had no particular identity; MISG funding was viewed as a grant from the local authority. Even the grant's perceived short-term nature was of no special interest to projects in the voluntary sector as time limited funding was a fact of life.

> **CO-ORDINATING PROJECT DEVELOPMENT**
>
> Successful ways of steering MISG development and keeping all the relevant agencies informed included:
>
> ∆ the appointment of a development officer in the SSD
> ∆ setting up an umbrella organisation for mental health which brought together all the agencies and groups concerned
> ∆ ensuring middle managers in health and social services understood the aims and objectives of MISG so that they could encourage and use projects appropriately.

8.16 A valuable role for MISG development workers was to curb competition where it would not be in the users' interests. Some MISG projects felt especially vulnerable as similar alternative services were available in the locality. They felt the alternative services could be competing with them for resources and the competition was not in the clients best interest—it neither encouraged interagency contact which would benefit clients nor did it promote quality care. Cost cutting would seriously erode the efficiency of some services which were inevitably expensive because they offered 24 hour care, 7 days a week and provided adequately for the support, and safety, of workers.

"One of the fears I have is being taken over by someone offering something similar cheaper." (**Team Leader**)

8.17 Success had undoubtedly created problems for some projects. In the last two years, as MISG has increased annually by little more than inflation, successful projects were suffering from growth in uptake and no matching growth in funding. Where this was combined with low turn over because the services were targeted on those with long-term needs, projects were feeling considerable pressure. The only ways found to cope with this were overspend, the operation of a waiting list or a loss of flexibility; all of which were unsatisfactory.

8.18 Pressure on services also led to unrealistic expectations being placed on workers. MISG projects had often been set up with minimum funding and very broad remits which were open to interpretation. As demand grew, it was very easy for committed workers to expand the scope of the project resulting in unrealistic workloads. This problem was made worse by:
- acute difficulties in recruiting volunteers in some areas
- the lack of alternative services
- the threat of the termination of temporary funding.

> **REASONABLE EXPECTATIONS?**
>
> One project was run by an organiser, who with the help of a sessional worker and volunteers:
>
> △ ran 2 weekly group meetings
> △ managed a monthly meeting for a voluntary organisation
> △ managed a volunteer visiting service
> △ assessed new referrals (34 between January and October 1994)
> △ visited clients at home who were causing concern to review the situation and refer on if necessary
> △ recruited and trained volunteers
> △ provides a telephone support and information service.
>
> Funding was for a single 24 hour a week part-time post.

INTERAGENCY ISSUES

8.19 MISG has been at the forefront of the development of services delivered by statutory, voluntary and private agencies, as well as by user and carer groups. As a result, interagency links have been crucial, not only at the planning stage, but also at the operational level.

Health

8.20 Joint decision making between SSDs and health authorities is an integral part of MISG policy. This is intended to ensure that the most effective use is made of health and social services resources and yet, relations between SSDs, health authorities, including FHSAs, varied enormously, ranging from excellent to unsatisfactory. MISG decision-making sometimes fitted into existing planning structures or was sometimes the catalyst which encouraged the creation of new arrangements. Overall, the necessity to collaborate over the allocation of MISG was felt to have been positive. At worst the involvement of the health authority had had little or no impact. No authorities had found the process a hindrance.

8.21 The development of joint commissioning, and the growth of locality planning, were expected to influence future MISG planning but these changes were too recent for their effects to have been felt in 1993/4.

Voluntary Sector

8.22 In all authorities visited, the voluntary sector played an important role in MISG provision and, in most authorities, it participated at the planning stage. However, it has been difficult for voluntary agencies to take a proactive stance concerning MISG and there were a number of reasons for this.

- In 1991 when the first year of the grant was allocated, the short time scale given for decisions to be made on MISG spending prevented widespread consultation in those authorities where forums for joint discussion were undeveloped or where complex structures existed, for example in counties where decision making had been devolved. Therefore, decisions on the initial use of MISG were sometimes made internally within the SSD. Although joint planning may have improved since, increases in MISG have remained small and so the scope for changing the expenditure pattern of the grant has been limited.

- MISG has tended to be given to known and established voluntary mental health agencies rather than to stimulate new ones. The system of submitting bids for the grant has encouraged this as success is dependent on knowing the system, hearing about the bidding process, being able to assure delivery of the service and LAs having confidence in the agency.

- Where new organisations, or new branches of existing organisations, have been developed specially to provide innovative services, or to plug gaps in services, the push tended to come from the SSD. Social services also usually provided management expertise and experience of service delivery in the initial stages to help the new agency to become established.

> **STIMULATING NEW PROJECTS: THE NEW COMMONWEALTH WOMEN'S MENTAL HEALTH PROJECT**
>
> The Women's Project is a social and therapeutic group for women from minority ethnic communities. It has been developed and managed by a Section 11 worker employed by the SSD but it comes under the umbrella of the Panjabi Centre which is a voluntary organisation established over 7 years ago. A major challenge facing the women's group is its move to complete independence in the Panjabi Centre and it is envisaged that it might be two years before the project is ready to become completely independent from social services managerial support and premises. Even then, it will remain in partnership with the SSD.

Private sector

8.23 Little use of the private sector was found, even in those authorities which had a political commitment to its development. However, there was evidence of increased involvement of private care organisations in the planning process and locality groups.

> **DEVELOPING AN INDEPENDENT COMPANY**
>
> The Club began as a health authority managed, pilot scheme with:
>
> *"6 people, 4 seconded part time staff and enough money from the health authority for tea, coffee and sandwiches."* (**Worker**)
>
> The workers built up the club through contacting people who had been users of the local day hospital which had closed. It was so popular that, at the end of the pilot period, the club was awarded a capital grant of £20,000 for building works and was funded for 2 years by MISG. Continuing its early success, at the end of this time, the SSD put the service out to contract and received three tenders, two from local voluntary organisations and one from the workers. After difficult negotiations, and the support of users, the Council agreed to offer the contract to the workers giving them a matter of weeks to form a company and prepare themselves take over.
>
> They formed a private company limited by guarantee; a non-profit making, spending company which meets the requirements of the local authority contract. Using MISG funding, this arrangement worked well until the company wanted to expand into its own premises. In order to own and maintain a building, the workers have been forced to set up a second company which can make a profit. This enables them to keep some reserve finance to meet the cost of upkeep and maintenance. Having sought advice, it has been decided no advantage would come from charitable status.

Housing

8.24 A number of the MISG projects which were visited worked in close association with local housing agencies in recognition of the importance of housing, and the recurring housing problems often experienced by people with long-term mental health problems. MISG workers were involved in supporting users in specially allocated furnished, and unfurnished, accommodation, managing group homes, staffing short-term accommodation and participating in a joint county SSD, housing and health service group to address the housing needs of people with mental illness.

> **HOMELESS PROJECT**
>
> The project manages three types of accommodation. Firstly, there is the hostel for single people who are homeless and mentally ill or have had problems related to substance abuse. It has capacity for 12 residents but 2 beds are kept for emergency use as it is staffed 24 hours a day. Secondly a block of self-contained flats has been renovated, furnished and fitted with the co-operation of the Housing Department. These flats are let to people with mental health problems but one is used as a community flat. The community flat is staffed between 9.00 am and 9.00 pm and provides a place where residents can meet together, get support and advice from the worker and have meals cooked. During the night, emergency cover is provided by the staff at the hostel.
>
> The third type of accommodation is a set of 5 flats which are rented by a housing association. The flats are furnished to a high standard and tenants are supervised by the project staff. Their length of stay is variable depending on how quickly they are ready to move on to their own accommodation.

Libraries

8.25 Co-operation between a local authority library services and MISG was found in one authority. It funded a mental health information service which was run in conjunction with the general information service provided in the city.

> **WORKING WITH A LIBRARY SERVICE: THE MENTAL HEALTH INFORMATION PROJECT**
>
> The Information Project was set up to enable clients of the Mental Health Support Workers Project to have easily accessible information about mental health in the city. It has since expanded to provide information to professionals, providers, clients and carers and it publishes a very successful quarterly newsletter. The project is located in the Information Centre in a city library and is closely associated with the city wide information service.

CPA

8.26 MISG was associated with the provision of social care for people on the Care Programme Approach (CPA) in the first explanation of the grant in the 1989 Community Care White Paper but, during the visits, no evidence of this type of link was identified. However, where CPA was working effectively, clear advantages for MISG projects were reported. These advantages stemmed from the formalising of interagency links imposed by CPA:

- project workers could have quick easy access to statutory authority services through the keyworker

> **BACK-UP FOR VOLUNTARY SECTOR PROVIDERS**
>
> Before the introduction of CPA, social workers were assessing clients, referring them to the Companion Service and then closing the case. This left the companions with a great deal of responsibility. Inevitably they were coming up with issues which the social workers couldn't be expected to uncover in their assessment visits and the Director was left to sort things out.
>
> *"It was wrong that we, as a provider organisation, should be left alone to support the clients. Our staff are only paid for their contact hours with clients; they are encouraged not to become too involved or to take work home with them."* (**Director**)

- independent sector workers were not left to cope in isolation with vulnerable people in the community without the back up they needed
- by contributing to CPA reviews, project workers felt that the knowledge of clients gained from their hands-on contact was used appropriately, and that they themselves were valued.

CPA concerns

8.27 Implementation of CPA remains patchy but the following issues were also identified which gave rise to concern:

- CPA and the role of keyworker were still not well understood in the majority of MISG projects, even in authorities where the policy had been implemented
- workers and clients had conflicting views as to who was on CPA, or what this meant
- it was reported that there was still some resistance by consultant psychiatrists to implementing CPA
- some health authorities were still piloting CPA and were not intending to implement the policy across the district until the pilot has been evaluated.

> **GOOD PRACTICE—CPA**
>
> A tool kit, containing the necessary information about CPA in the area, has been developed and supplied to all staff working in or with mental health throughout the authority.
>
> The Community Health Care NHS Trust and SSD have pooled resources to provide a single point of entry to specialist mental health services and an overall mental health service manager. This has resulted in a dramatic fall in waiting times, full implementation of CPA and the development of a MISG funded 7 day per week support service.
>
> A CPA Co-ordinator has responsibility for producing a digest of information collated from individual CPA records and this information is used for service planning purposes.

Care management

8.28 As with CPA, MISG projects were finding care management very helpful in those authorities where the system was working well. The main advantages were;

- it gave project workers access to the support and advice of a professional. The care manager was usually a social worker, and often an approved social worker, and so their involvement with, and knowledge of, a client was invaluable.

- project workers were able to act as advocates for clients at care management reviews giving them the confidence to speak their minds.

> **EXAMPLE OF MISG PROJECT INVOLVEMENT IN CARE MANAGEMENT REVIEWS**
>
> The workers take responsibility for setting up the 3 monthly reviews with the care managers, and anyother people involved. The worker will discuss the review with the client beforehand to prepare them but nothing is written down because clients tend to become suspicious. At reviews, the worker makes sure he/she is sitting beside the client to reassure them and to make it easier to act as advocate for them if needs be. This often takes the form of reminding clients of the things they mentioned earlier, for example. 'Did you want to tell the doctor about your medication or would you like me to say what you told me'.

- care management gave access to a budget which enabled services to adjust to a client's changing circumstances, including the funding of increased input by the MISG project through spot contracting

Care management issues

8.29 It was found that the introduction of care management has given rise to the following concerns:

- some authorities had not linked care management to CPA. CPA was seen to be the responsibility of health while care management was the responsibility of social services

- mental health social workers were redeployed into care management leaving a gap in social work provision which non-mental health professionals in MISG projects felt they were having to fill without always having had appropriate training for the work being done

- social workers were expected to adopt the purchasing role with little or no training

- care managers were acting as gate keepers to projects so preventing self-referrals and hindering referrals from sources such as GPs who could only refer via a care manager. This system was operating for some projects funded entirely by MISG where no recourse to the care management budget was involved.

- some in-house MISG projects were excluded from care management reviews because it was assumed that their internal review system was adequate.

- access to care management budgets was uneven throughout some county areas

- workers in the voluntary sector were not always invited to participate in reviews concerning their clients even when they were the main providers in the care package.

"I feel very isolated in the voluntary sector. I feel like a poor cousin. They do not recognise the contribution our service makes to individual care. We are part of care packages but are not invited to reviews and don't even feed into reviews—they have stopped asking us. They just phone up and say, 'Can you send Mrs Smith a volunteer please, I think this.........'." **(Organiser)**

USER INVOLVEMENT

8.30 The involvement of service users in the planning, management and delivery of service is promoted throughout official guidance to community care. In the monitoring visits, involvement was found at four levels. It was found at the levels of:
- strategic planning
- locality planning
- MISG projects
- individual care plans.

Strategic planning

8.31 The value of including the perspective of users and carers in the planning of services was certainly being recognised but many authorities were having difficulty in turning intention into practice. Even the most active authorities were still dissatisfied with what had been achieved. The effectiveness of this participation was very difficult to measure, but elements of good practice were identified. These included:
- financial and practical support and advice for user groups;
- 'Working together' days for key mental health stakeholders;
- specific planning days for members of minority ethnic communities;
- research involving users and carers to ensure development reflects locally felt need.

A USERS' GROUP

The Users Group was established by a few committed survivors with the encouragement of professionals who were concerned to see effective user participation develop in the city. With the help of a development grant for offices costs, and members expenses, the Group has formed an effective organisation which acts as an umbrella group for separate user forums running within mental health services such as day centres.

It has probably been most active in trying to set up a crisis service provided partially by survivors, but they have also achieved:

- running workshops for survivors on specific issues such as crisis support, employment
- training professionals
- involvement in planning meetings
- providing advocacy for patients at the long stay hospital
- presenting workshops at conferences
- running a road show
- supporting other survivor groups and paying grants to groups.

Concerns at strategic level

8.32 Concerns raised about involvement at this level were:
- its effectiveness

"We attended a consultative meeting where lots of notes were taken but nothing came of it."
- older people were not invited or encouraged to join planning discussions
- the black and minority communities were rarely being reached
- involvement was often through surveys rather than on-going discussion or participation

- confusion over the parallel planning processes now in place - consultation and involvement in the community care planning was well developed in some authorities, and users were found to be confused as to whether they were contributing to mental health strategies or community care plans. Were these the same thing, or were the key decisions now being made by joint purchasing groups from which they were excluded?

Locality planning

8.33 In authorities where locality planning was being established, users of MISG services were being encouraged to take part. MISG projects explained it was important for their users to be represented, both to ensure the process succeeded, and to keep the project informed of what takes place. However the process was still new:

"I have been to one meeting and will continue going. Its early days yet, I haven't worked out quite what happens."

Project level

8.34 It was found to be common practice to encourage users to become involved in committees within MISG projects, or in providing feedback on their experience of the service. This was obviously easier in projects where users regularly meet together in a centre, group or activity, but ways had been found to obtain the opinions of the users of home based services. User committees set up within projects were found to be both structured and unstructured, and achieved varying degrees of success, but it was pointed out that for many projects, the process of setting up and running a users committee was as important as the outcome. The models of user committees found are discussed further in paragraphs 7.7.

Individual care planning

8.35 In projects which involved individual care planning, good practice was found concerning the involvement of users and carers at the stages of assessment and negotiation of the care plans but less consistency was found at the review stage Projects which systematically obtained user and carer views at reviews, and fed this information back to the SSD planning and development section, were to be commended.

QUALITY AND MONITORING ISSUES

8.36 The overall impression, given by referrers and service users at the MISG projects visited, was that they were providing a very satisfactory quality of service. Many of the services were commended for their innovative, thoughtful and relevant approach. Some projects were felt to have had notable results and exciting potential.

Measuring quality

8.37 Very variable awareness of measuring quality was found ranging from projects which had a complete lack of quality standards to a project with a very structured and systematically quality assured system. A clear need was found for:

- further work by planners and operational staff on the development of quality standards
- work on methods of measuring whether standards have been adequately reached
- the building in of quality issues to staff training and supervision.

Contracts 8.38 It was found that the use of contracts and service level agreements was patchy although the need for them was being increasingly recognised by purchasers and providers alike. However, severe limitations were identified in the existing contracting arrangements such as:
- quality standards included in service level agreements were not made specific and tended to be limited to basic principles and good practice
- in-house providers in SSDs were not receiving service level agreements
- spot contracts neither specified service levels nor standards of output.

Evaluation 8.39 As many MISG projects have pioneered new approaches to the support of mentally ill people living in the community, it was expected that projects would be thoroughly researched and yet evaluations were rare. The evaluations which were found tended to be:
- specified for pilot projects but not always carried out
- expected by MISG grant givers without clarity as to how it should be carried out, by whom or when
- unsophisticated and not a basis for further work
- heavily reliant on user feedback.

Monitoring 8.40 Systematic monitoring was largely undeveloped. Many projects were subject to regular reviews, one authority maintaining a three yearly cycle of minor and major review for each project. Difficulties encountered with monitoring were:
- commitment was not matched by progress
- project managers were responsible for monitoring but often had little time and expertise to give to setting up systems and ensuring they ran
- where workable and effective monitoring systems were found, they were likely to be the result of a research study, such as an evaluation
- heavy dependence was placed on an annual questionnaire obtaining users' views
- complex computer systems were being developed but had not been completed
- senior managers or MISG co-ordinators often had to take responsibility for progress reviews instead of MISG staff.

CONCLUSIONS

9

Prior findings

9.1 The review of the literature on MISG up to 1993 indicated that the achievements of the grant were considerable with large number of projects established. These services were characterised by innovation, flexibility and informality, and they placed a new emphasis on the value of involving service users in their planning and delivery. The grant had also stimulated joint work and new partnerships. Useful experience had been gained in contractual relationships.

9.2 Despite this activity, serious gaps remained in service provision for the severely mentally ill and little, or no, attempt had been made to link MISG to CPA at a strategic level. Other concerns were that strategic planning remained patchy and was severely limited by undeveloped needs assessment, and a lack of management and financial information in SSDs.

Achievements

9.3 The 1993/4 monitoring study echoed many of these findings. The principle achievements of MISG were the amount of activity generated by the grant and the shift away from a building based, service led approach to responsive services accessible during traditionally anti-social hours. A very diverse range of projects had been welcomed by their users who, prior to the service commencing, often had had no effective form of support. Many of these projects were pioneering new ways of providing support, often with very specialist, yet non-professional, workers and new models of partnerships with users.

Strengths

9.4 The strength of MISG has been its role in stimulating growth in an previously underdeveloped service area at a time of widespread economic constraint in the public sector. Its broad criteria have encouraged considerable innovation in response to the demands and assessed needs of users leading to projects with highly motivated and enthusiastic staff. Largely due to staff commitment, MISG services have been extremely successful in supporting people at home, including very ill people, and ensuring hospital admissions are appropriate.

9.5 In some cases MISG projects have been developed alongside care management and CPA. Where these systems are working well, and are integrated to support a whole network of care, MISG projects in both the statutory and independent sectors can play an important role, delivering a service, feeding into reviews and alerting systems when the need arises.

9.6 Joint work had also been stimulated by MISG with projects working collaboratively with other agencies. These relationships were rarely formalised but did a great deal to ensure information, skills and resources which were available in the statutory sector, were shared with voluntary sector workers and users, and vice versa. Particularly encouraging were the development of links with housing and health, and recognition of the contribution users can make to service planning, delivery and review.

Weaknesses 9.9 The main weakness of MISG was found to be the perceived uncertainty of its funding and the obstacles in the way of its strategic use. These included the lack of strategic planning, the under-development of needs assessment and the complexities of joint commissioning. At project level, a major concern was the lack of accountability arising from inadequate monitoring and identification of measurable standards. For many projects, problems were also being created by the patchy implementation of care management and CPA.

Lessons 9.10 MISG has shown that successful community mental health services do not have to be large or costly. What they need to do is constantly explore, with users and carers, the best ways in which needs can be met. Much good practice has been developed and users are becoming very effective in getting their voices heard.

9.11 If gaps in services are to be avoided, and an effective mixed market of care is to be developed, a strategic approach to planning the use of MISG spending should be adopted, based on thorough consideration of local need. MISG has already proved successful in going some way to meeting that need but there is still a long way to go before people with mental illness will be adequately supported in the community.

PROJECT STUDY

1

DAY CLUB FOR ADULTS IN THE INDEPENDENT SECTOR

"RENDEZVOUS" CLUB 70, KIRKLEES

'Rendezvous' Club 70 is a very successful social centre for people experiencing the long-term effects of mental illness. It was established by the health authority following the closure of the local hospital but is run now by a private company under a contractual agreement with the Social Services Department. For the last four years it has been based in a youth club and run 4 days a week but it has now moved to its own building and hopes to be able to respond to its members' request for more flexible opening.

The Club provides a friendly relaxed place for members to spend the day, meet their friends, eat an inexpensive meal and have the opportunity to talk and seek advice about things concerning them. It also engages members in fund-raising so that they can go on outings, enjoy holidays together and share celebrations. Additional benefits from the club include preventative work by the workers when members are be becoming unwell, providing advice and support, linking in with other services where necessary and even offering a telephone help line. The popularity of the club can be seen from the numbers who attend and this is largely due to the commitment and energy of the staff.

Pilot The Club began as a pilot project but, because of the workers' success in building it up, in 1991, it was awarded a capital grant of £20,000 to do up the building and was funded for 2 years from the mental Illness Specific Grant (MISG).

The contract At the end of the pilot in 1991 Kirklees SSD put the service out for tender and after negotiations, supported by the club members, the workers were awarded the contract. They had just a matter of weeks to form a company and prepare themselves take over responsibility for every aspect of the service.

The company They formed a private company limited by guarantee; a non-profit making spending company which is currently funded by MISG. The grant meets the day-to-day running expenses of the club but all extra activities are funded by money collected by members through fund-raising. £2,100 was raised between April and October 1994, the annual target being about £4,500. This is kept in the members bank account and spent by them on outings, holidays and celebrations; a key part of the club's activities.

Staffing The club is managed by the two owners and they run it with the assistance of one worker. The club is currently only open 4 days a week, but is moving to new premises where it will be open on 6 days.

Project Study

Criteria The club is for people with long-term mental health problems and referrals come from a wide range of sources including social work, probation, the youth hostel, the Day Resource Centre, Richmond Fellowship and MIND. All members must have a key workers from health or social services to whom the club workers can refer if they are concerned.

Members' likes

Friendship	Everybody gets on	A big family
Understanding	A meal	Stigma free
Caring	The workers	Being able to talk
Confidentiality	Looking forward	Holidays and trips

GOOD PRACTICE

Values When the club was set up, it established groundrules based on the 'standards and values held by 'ordinary people'.; *"what you would find in a working man's club because we didn't want to appear institutionalised."* (Worker)

Trust is important because *"We can't have people who we cannot trust not to steal. The club runs very much on trust and it works."* (Worker). These values have also helped to ensure that there is no 'us and them' attitude between staff and members.

Monitoring and support One of the most important roles of the workers is to pre-empt crisis by watching for signs of someone having problems or becoming ill. The workers also maintain what amounts to a telephone help line to support people getting into difficulties when the club is closed. They claim this line is rarely abused.

CPA CPA is also helping workers to monitor their members. In recognition of the support given at the club, workers are invited to feed verbally into CPA reviews and are occasionally invited to attend review meetings if there is general concern about a member. They do so willingly and find the involvement helpful. If anything is asked about members which workers regard as confidential, they will seek the member's agreement before disclosing the information.

Family involvement The club not only welcomes the involvement of families, but the workers like to get to know relatives and to understand home circumstances. Workers also try to support families and to help them understand mental illness. Members are also invited to take their family and friends on holiday with them as there are many advantages; everybody gets to know one another better in relaxing circumstances, carers get a holiday and it can be financially advantageous to take a bigger party.

Involvement The club has a members committee which meets monthly to plan activities. There is also a Steering Group which had members of health, social services, police and two representatives from the club.

ISSUES

The issues currently facing the club are:

Understanding A lack of understanding by other agencies of the pressures of working in a small independent organisation. The club is compared to two other day services provided locally but neither of these services caters for between 30 and 40 members a day providing activities, support, advice and a hot meal with just 3 staff. At the same time the workers run the business, pay the wages, keep the books, supply the club, arrange holidays for members and provide a 24 hour crisis line. Recently they have also been developing a large new social centre which they are moving into without a day's closure. They do not have any relief staff who could step in and run the club for a day while they attend meetings.

"We are all playing a ball game but they are playing football and we are playing rugby."

Training Similarly the workers are unable to attend training events and so find it difficult to keep abreast community care changes. Yet they need the information and they have to trust the statutory sector to supply it.

Funding Being dependent on MISG does give cause for concern as no other funding source has been discussed. Yet the workers have been assured that their funding will be found and the provision of the capital required for the new building by the local authority would appear to support this optimism. However, the workers have been invited to join a Consortium of voluntary projects which will look at ways of accessing fund and they are happy to participate.

Project Study

PROJECT STUDY

2

VOLUNTARY SECTOR DAY CENTRE

WELLINGTON STREET DAY CENTRE, NORTHAMPTON

Wellington Street Day Centre is named after the street in which it is situated in the centre of Northampton. It was set up in 1989 to support people being discharged from hospital but, since then, it has begun to welcome people with mental health problems from anywhere within the local community. The principle aims of the Centre are to build up people's confidence and social networks, help them make use of community facilities, link with other support services and look for ways of working jointly with other services offered by MIND. The Centre is open 4 days a week for day centre activities and once a week for one-to-one sessions to help members with specific problems. It has about 60 members with up to 30 attending on each day.

Staffing   Wellington Street is staffed by a full-time manager, a part-time assistant (18 hours) and sessional workers (25 hours). In addition, volunteers and member/volunteers help to run the Centre and form part of the staff group, attending staff meetings and taking part in staff development sessions.

Activities   It is an informal service which offers a range of activities including a Women's Group, Book Club and Music Club. Every summer a holiday is arranged and members have been abroad together.

Food   Tea and coffee can be brought throughout the day and a lunch is cooked.

Shared plans   Members participate in organising the Centre at a fortnightly Community Meeting to which all staff, volunteers and members are invited. In addition, on alternate fortnights, an Advocacy Meeting is run at Wellington Street by the Users Support Service, a Mental Health Advocacy Project at which members can discuss things which are bothering them at home, or the Centre.

Funding   The Centre was originally funded by the Health Authority but in 1991, it received some additional funding from Joint Finance as part of Northampton Social Services 30% contribution to MISG. This grant has now expired. However last year the service was fully funded by the SSD and Health jointly. This year the service was funded through the Authority's overall arrangements with MIND. Any future expansion of the service will need to be negotiated between the Centre and the local authority.

Members' likes	The people	Company	Someone to talk to
	Location	The garden	People with similar illnesses
	Activities	Flexibility	Food
	Way treated	Help and support	Self help
	Volunteers	Staff help	

GOOD PRACTICE

Individual support As staff have little time while the Centre is open to give members individual attention, they take the opportunity on Fridays, when the Centre is closed, to work with members on their own. Members may need help or advice or may receive training in living skills to help them live more independently. Workers also visit members at home.

Involvement in the Centre The Community Meeting gives members a say in what is going on. They discuss the programme and activities, holiday plans and outings. It is also an opportunity to discuss how things are going and to exchange information. *"It tells us what's going on. It is both ways. It is very helpful. Everybody has a say here. You have to be reasonable about it."*

The Advocacy Meeting offers members the opportunity to discuss much broader issues without the workers of the Centre being present. Information from these meetings is only fed back to the staff if the members choose to do so.

Meals A member/volunteer provides inexpensive tea and coffee throughout the day at the centre. Lunch is cooked daily by a part-time cook with some assistance from members but the kitchen facilities are too small for members to do much more than the clearing up. Lunch is a very social part of the day.

Involvement in wider mental health issues Members are enthusiastic about attending conferences and mental health planning meetings. One MIND member also attends the MIND conferences and feeds back to the group. Contact with other MIND services is encouraged with visits organised to neighbouring MIND groups.

Links with other services Workers at Wellington Street will assist members to use health and social services as appropriate, and they liaise with other mental health professionals if they are concerned about a members. This is important as many members feel: *"I can always talk to the staff here when I don't feel like talking to other help."*

Members do use other mental health services but recognise Wellington Street is different: *"Other services are more structured—here you don't need to do anything if you don't feel like it."*

Project Study

ISSUES

Building The building is liked for its space and location in the town centre but it is shared and the landlords place severe limitations on the way the project can use the premises; everything has to be cleared up everyday and the notice board has to be hidden after use. Also the size of the kitchen prevents members from using it except on a one-to-one basis for cookery training. A new building is being sought but uncertain funding makes planning difficult.

More young members Some members feel the Centre should target more young people as most of the members are between the age of 30 and 70. They feel young people tend to be more motivated and could provide more energy for activities. The lack of men staff was also felt to be a regret by some members.

Mini-bus When the mini-bus had to be scrapped, the project was unable to replace it and its loss is felt strongly by members. It not only helped to bring members in to the Centre but was also used for trips out. Only one or two members have been unable to attend the Centre without the provision of transport but the mini bus is missed for the many small excursion to places such as garden centres and out-of-town shops in particular. Having to hire transport also puts up the cost of holidays and trips.

Funding One of the most important issues members would like to influence and change is the funding of the Centre. The funding structure is not easy to understand and members resent the fact that, although funding comes through the statutory sector, the Centre is under-resourced compared to statutory services. On top of that members have to help with MIND collections.

ISSUES MENTIONED BY MEMBERS
- Landlords and landladies take too much money.
- Should services for people with health problems be segregated? Does this help members to mix in community activities as community care intends?
- Ignorance of mental illness: *"The difficulty is ignorance. People who look different are not treated right in the community. There is too much ignorance."*

PROJECT STUDY

3

HOME BASED SERVICE

THE COMMUNITY SUPPORT TEAM, MILTON KEYNES, BUCKINGHAMSHIRE

The Community Support Team is a 24 hour service for people living in Milton Keynes with long-term mental health problems. It was set up by the Social Services Department and it provides a range of services including on-going support, rehabilitation, help in emergencies and crisis intervention.

The aim of the team is to help clients develop their ability to cope with living independently in the community with their illness. The workers support people with friendship, advice, encouragement, access to other services and training in every day living skills such as shopping, cooking and socialising. This support is given 7 days a week if needed and visits are made more than once a day if a client becomes unwell or has difficulties. In emergencies, the emergency services will call the team out so that clients receive help from someone they know and who knows them. The success of the service is very dependent on the skills and commitment of the workforce it has and the very thorough back-up systems that are in place.

History   The Community Support Team was initially set up with rehabilitation officers (RO), but, in 1991, MISG was used to fund 3 additional community support workers (CSW) posts. It was intended that these workers would cover weekend and evening work and sleep-overs when required so ensuring a 24 hour service, 7 days a week but, in practice, there was little demand for sleep-overs and the team has been restructured to dovetail into the Buckinghamshire model for care management.

Team   The team consists of 6 ROs for mental health and 3 CSWs. It also currently includes ROs for physical disability and it will soon have staff who will work exclusively with older people with mental health problems. Overall, the focus is on adults with long-term mental ill health.

Resource Centre   The team is located in a mental health resource centre which provides day care for adults and older people and an office base for the Community Support Team and a mental health social work team. The social work team is now responsible for care management but still provides approved social work cover and works closely with the Support Team.

Rehabilitation Officers   The ROs carry about 15 cases each. They are responsible for assessment and establishing individual care plans for clients with the care manager. They will set up the care plan and see it through, bringing in a CSW if a piece of planned work is needed, for

Project Study

example, helping someone with their shopping or teaching budgeting, money management or cooking. The RO provide on-going support and, although they are not trained social workers, all have experience of work in the mental health field and fulfil much of the traditional social work role They are supervised by the Senior Rehabilitation Officer.

Community Support Workers Two of the CSWs work full-time and the third post is a job share. Each CSW is supervised by a particular RO but can work with any member of the team. Since the recent restructuring, the full-time workers will work alternate weekends. On Saturdays they will visit clients who are causing concern, and do planned work with clients who find weekends very lonely times. On Sundays they will carry out planned visits in the morning and spend the afternoon in a Drop-In to encourage clients to come out rather than be visited.

GOOD PRACTICE

24 hour cover The team is accessible for clients on a 24 hour basis. Occasionally sleep-ins are needed and the CSW will stay with a client over night but care is taken not to let this service be abused. Although the team is not a blue light service, it responds to emergencies and is well known to the emergency duty team and the police. By knowing the client and their illness, the team can calm situations and ensure appropriate response is obtained. They can prevent unnecessary hospital admissions or, if admission is required, they may be able to persuade the client to go in voluntarily.

Weekend work The Team continues to support vulnerable clients throughout the weekend. Weekend visits are planned at the weekly team meeting and care is taken to hand over all relevant information.

Home based Most of the work undertaken by the team is home based with workers going to see clients in their homes and working both preventatively and proactively from there. This approach reinforces the individuality of the support given to each client and the flexibility which the team offers.

Teamwork Support of this demanding client group 7 days a week is only possible with good teamwork. The team get to know each others' clients and clients get to know the whole team. This reduces dependency on particular workers and increases the effectiveness of the team.

Supervision The team is mutually supportive but there is also a well planned system for staff supervision and support. Overall case responsibility is held by the social worker/care manager.

A great deal of consideration is given to staff safety with clear procedures agreed on how to handle situations such as potentially dangerous clients, threatened overdoses and aggression.

Case reviews The ROs are responsible for ensuring that care plans are reviewed 3 monthly. They will discuss the review with the client beforehand to prepare them and will act as advocate if necessary.

Planned work The CSWs provide a key role within the team in ensuring programmed work and training with clients takes place as planned.

Group homes The team works closely with housing agencies and to help clients to cope independently, they have set up a number of group homes each housing 2 to 3 residents. They also manage a block of flats in which accommodation is let to clients who receive the support of ROs.

7 to 9 Club The opportunity for clients to meet together socially is provided by an evening social club (named the 7 to 9 Club by a member). The club is run by a CSW.

ISSUES

Adjustment to care management With care management taking up more and more of the time of the mental health social work team, which inevitably has had a knock on effect upon the work of the Rehabilitation Officers and the community support team, the ongoing support of Rehabilitation Officers for people assessed through care management in their own homes and in homely settings in their community is essential. The role of the Rehabilitation Officer is currently subject to a county wide review.

Contracting If, and when, all services have to be contracted, it is difficult to see how anything but a block contract would give the Support Team the flexibility it needs to continue providing the individual, and fluctuating, care it does today. It is also to be hoped that such services will be able to stay within the statutory sector as it is difficult to envisage an independent agency providing the professionalism of the Support Team with the strong back-up and support arrangements for staff together with the links with housing

Boundaries A major issue for the Support Team is the ill defined boundary between mental health services and those for people with learning disabilities. The team supports people with behavioural problems who have been rejected by other services because of their difficult behaviour. The Support Team will take on the care of the clients even though they can have a very destructive influence and the team is continually having to look for new solutions for them.

Project Study

PROJECT STUDY

4

HOME BASED SERVICE

THE MENTAL HEALTH SUPPORT TEAM, SALFORD

In Salford, the majority of MISG has been used to develop the Mental Health Support Team, but, to enhance the effectiveness of this team, the grant has also funded a series of smaller projects. As these smaller projects were set up to focus their activities on the clients of the Support Team, the MISG investment has traditionally been regarded as a single development.

Support Team   The Mental Health Support Team is a domiciliary service which provides practical and emotional care and support to people with severe mental health problems. It arose from research carried out on how MISG should be spent and aims to adopt an informal and flexible approach to working with clients in order to meet their individual needs and help people to help themselves as much as possible using local support. Run by the Social Services Department, the team works within the area covered by three of the Department's Community Teams.

The team consists of 13 support workers, a senior support worker, an administrator, a part-time psychologist and a part-time occupational therapist. They are all based in an office at Pendleton but work as three smaller patch teams linking in with the local multi-disciplinary mental health teams. Most referrals come from these Community Mental Health teams.

Criteria   The team supports people aged 18 to 65 with serious mental health problems. All referrals go through the care management system to ensure they are officially logged onto the social services referral system.

Goal planning   Clients are introduced to the Support Team by the referrer and their needs are identified. The support worker then negotiates with the client how they would like these need to be met. To confirm this, a goal planning meeting is held to clarify with all concerned what the support worker will do and what is intended. These decisions are then reviewed at the next goal planning meeting to assess what has been achieved and what is best to do next.

Other MISG projects associated with the Support Team:

MIND Advocacy Worker: Salford MIND was funded to provide advocacy for clients of the Support Team but, as demand was low, the worker widened the brief to develop advocacy generally in Salford.

Family Support Worker: Making Space were funded for a worker to work with the families of clients of the Support Team. Again, the role of the worker has broadened in response to demand.

Homeless Initiative: Information about services for people who are homeless and have a mental health problem was made available at the Salford Cathedral Centre Drop-in.

START Project Worker: Arising from the Kings Fund Centre project, Better Futures, an art worker has been employed to work with Support Team clients and others to develop their confidence in creative work and to use these skills to undertake contract work and commissioned art work in the community.

MIND'S Sunday Drop-in: A small grant was given to the Sunday drop-in run by MIND in recognition of the need to encourage weekend services.

Salford Users Group: A few very committed survivors have formed an effective organisation which acts as an umbrella group for separate user forums running within mental health services such as day centres. Through its varied activities, the Group has gained considerable recognition ensuring the involvement of survivors in the planning, training and the delivery of services. They also manage a small budget funded by MISG, with which they can provide start-up funding for new user groups.

Information Service: An information project was set up to enable clients of the Support Team to have easily accessible information about mental health in Salford. The project is located in the Information Centre in a city library and is closely associated with the city wide information service. It publishes a quarterly newsletter on up to date events in mental health in Salford.

Client likes	Everything	Confidence	Company	Friendship
	A new face	Looking forward	Choices	Flexibility
	Support	Talking	Go places	Goal planning

GOOD PRACTICE

Training To ensure the support workers are appropriately and adequately trained, a training course was devised giving workers a City and Guild qualification in developing a mental health service. This has since been changed to a programme which could support an NVQ.

Flexibility Clients value the way the support they received can be stepped up or down depending on how well they are. They also appreciated being able to change their support worker not so much because clients don't get on with them but because, after a while both worker and client can benefit from a change. *"I like any flexibility and freedom we have of choice so we can keep our individuality and not be labelled."*

Special interests Support workers bring special skills and attributes to the job and which can be used in working with clients. Care is taken to match workers and clients at the outset and to involve the most appropriate worker as, and when, needed. Workers also run some group activities such as gardening. The choice of activity, and the frequency and duration of visits, is negotiated directly between the client and the support worker.

Client involvement The participation of clients in deciding the overall direction of the service is more difficult as the project is home-based but 6-monthly client consultation meetings are held to which all clients are invited. At the request of clients, opinions are also collected through questionnaires and meetings are held to discuss the results.

The Salford User Group is another source of client opinion, but its activities span a much wider remit than commenting on services. They have been most active in trying to set up a crisis service provided partially by survivors and have successfully gained recognition and acceptance from the professional community as well as survivors and carers.

Information Clients are kept informed of what is going on through the mental health newsletter titled **MAROONED**. It has a fast growing circulation being distributed to clients, ex-clients, professionals, services and voluntary sector agencies.

ISSUES

Competition The team is working to full capacity and has been forced to operate a waiting list. As a result, two similar services have been developed in the independent sector which care managers are now buying in order to offer clients support. While the Support Team is funded by MISG it has the advantage that its services are free of charge to care managers, but this advantage could be lost if MISG funding ended. Then, the Support Team would be at a disadvantage in competing for contract as it is a statutory sector service and the care management budget must be spent in the independent sector.

Short-term involvement The Support Team works with clients for a limited period as it is felt that as many clients as possible should have the benefit of short-term input in order to maximise its effectiveness. When clients are well enough, the team gradually withdraws but up until now they have been able to keep an open door for people who have moved on, offering them a way back if it is needed. This is appreciated by ex-clients but they feel the team is now so busy there is little time left for them.

Flexibility With the growing workload, the Support Team is loosing some of its flexibility, particularly its ability to adjust schedules for the changing needs of clients. With encouragement from clients to introduce evening and weekend support, pressure on workers could increase.

PROJECT STUDY

GROUP FOR MINORITY ETHNIC WOMEN

NEW COMMONWEALTH WOMEN'S MENTAL HEALTH PROJECT, REDBRIDGE

The women's mental health project was set up in January 1992 using underspend from MISG. It aimed to provide support for women from minority ethnic communities who had experienced mental health problems and who found existing support services inappropriate for reasons of language and/or culture. Since then the group has grown and developed, successfully providing the women with social contact, therapeutic activities and new opportunities.

The group meets weekly but so strong is the women's commitment to the group that they often meet outside these sessions. As a result participation in the project has helped the women enormously. They have become better able to cope at home and relapses leading to hospital admission have been prevented. Some of the members have become well enough to take up jobs and one woman has completed a course in counselling so that she can now help others in the way she wished to be helped herself.

The idea for the group originated 3 years ago as staff became aware that the then new social services mental health day service was not reaching women from the ethnic minorities. One of the reasons that women felt unable to use the day facilities was because there were men there, but also, no staff came from their culture and no-one spoke their language. As a result, these women were being discharged from hospital, being visited at home for a while by nurses who administered medication and then not being heard of again until they relapsed. The support group was proposed to intercept this pattern.

A member of staff, Kiran Juttla, employed by the SSD, under Section 11 of the Local Government Act 1986, was asked to research and set up the group. She found widespread support for the proposal and was successful in obtaining funding.

Catchment   The group is open to all women from the New Commonwealth who now live in the London Borough of Redbridge.

Independent   The project comes under the umbrella of the Panjabi Centre, a voluntary organisation which has been running for over 7 years in Redbridge. The Panjabi Centre is independent of the Social Services Department but it receives managerial support from the Section 11 officer.

Premises   Meetings of the women's group take place in the mental health day centre and all its facilities are open to the women including an art therapy room, computer room and music room. These premises have two main advantages; first they are very pleasant and secondly they are culturally neutral, no specific group feeling more at home than any other.

Staff The group has two workers. The Section 11 officer is responsible for the development of the group and its overall management. In this work, her knowledge of mental health gained from a qualification in psychology has been particularly valuable. The group is run by a sessional worker who has had some training in basic counselling skills. Both workers speak the community languages of some group members and have been with the group since it began.

Finance Although the initial funding for the group was just £350 from Redbridge MISG underspend in 1991/2, the budget had risen to £12,000 for 1994/5. This has enabled the group to effectively buy in more therapeutic activities and move from being a social group to being one in which the women are positively encouraged and assisted to use appropriate help.

Criteria Referral are restricted to people who have used specialist psychiatric services. In practice, this means coming through the hospital system in some way.

Group activities The group meets from 1.00-3.30 pm every Tuesday. Women who are not able to drive themselves, or make their own way in, are provided with transport which starts its pick up at 12 noon. The sessional worker accompanies the women as an escort and Redbridge Volunteer Bureau—Community Transport Service provide the mini-bus.

Activities during the meeting vary but the primary need for social time is recognised. Every meeting begins with exercises and therapeutic sessions are usually run in blocks or at regular intervals, for example a stress management course was run for 6 weeks and a counsellor comes in once a month. Outings are arranged. Recently a group therapy session has proved very beneficial a second weekly meeting has been arranged to enable members, who are interested, to focus on group therapy.

Members' likes Get help   Get on well   Supportive
                   Looking forward Talking out   Removes loneliness

"You get relaxed from coming here. You can talk about whatever you like to the group. Once you go home, it's finished so you can look forward to cooking or whatever. It helps. I am looking forward to Tuesdays all the time."

Project Study

GOOD PRACTICE

Women only One of the most important characteristics of the group is that it is run by and for women. "You still need the women's thing. We can relate to women better."

Mixed culture While the group is exclusively for women from the New Commonwealth, this includes Asian, Chinese and Afro-Caribbean women. The organisers faced a great deal of scepticism at first as to whether such a mixed cultural group could succeed but now, "We feel confident that culture need not be an issue"(Worker). Members identify themselves as ethnic community women, not Black or Asian and the different cultural backgrounds have enriched the group.

Language Language plays an important part. The workers ensure the participation of all the women in the group by talking with women in their own language and interpreting group discussions. This particularly helps those on heavy medication who have difficulty being motivated to speak in English. The ability to train in the appropriate languages can also be of huge benefit.

Transport Transport to and from meetings is vital as many of the women feel unable to use public transport. Also, it helps to provide reassurance and give women whose motivation is low the incentive to go out. The problem with the transport is that it is expensive and its limited capacity is now committed to existing members so enforcing new members to find their own way to the group.

Open group One of the strengths of the group is its openness. The women welcome new members knowing how much they themselves have needed and benefited from the group.

Involvement The women in the group have the opportunity to discuss any proposed activities or changes to the group although they do not have any involvement in the management of the group.

Links The workers keep in touch with members social workers, CPNs and doctors at the request of the women concerned and often find themselves advocating on the women's behalf. If a worker is concerned about a woman, she may contact another professional who is involved in the woman's care without prior agreement, but the contact will be recorded on file and members can see their files whenever they wish.

ISSUES

The issues raised by the group were:
- the lack of services for women in Redbridge from the New Commonwealth with mental health problems particularly those with young children who need crèche facilities

- the uncertainties of MISG funding
- the move to complete independence in the voluntary sector under the wing of the Panjabi Centre.

Project Study

PROJECT STUDY 6

GROUP FOR PEOPLE EXPERIENCING LOSS

CONNECT GROUP, DERBYSHIRE

In North East Derbyshire, MISG has been used to develop an effective interagency service for people with long-term mental health needs. It has strengthened two multi-disciplinary mental health teams and supported five Community Support Workers who work with people in their own homes and out in the community. They have also set up a range of groups to help people with specific difficulties, one of which is CONNECT providing social contact and mutual support for people who have experienced loss

Community Support Workers The Community Support Workers Project provides hands-on support for people experiencing long-term mental health problems aged between 17 and 70. The workers are based in community mental health teams at Clay Cross and Killamarsh and they work closely with other team members providing support in people's homes, helping people get out and about and supporting people in crisis. Most referrals come from GPs, the hospital and social services, but self-referrals are welcomed. All new referrals are visited by a support worker together with a Community Psychiatric Nurse to assess how their needs can best be met and whether the support workers can help.

The involvement of the support workers is usually planned for about 6 months and during that time they often work with the CPNs and social workers in the team to ensure a client's care programme is maintained. As support workers tend to be the workers who get to know clients best, their contribution to care programme reviews is valued and they attend the reviews with clients whenever possible.

Because of the short-term nature of support workers involvement with clients, they encourage clients to take part in groups which have been set up to provide on-going support. Nine groups are currently running, including groups for older people, young people with schizophrenia, survivors of sexual abuse, women experiencing mental distress.

CONNECT is a group for people who have experienced loss and bereavement in NE Derbyshire. It has grown into a group of 12 people who meet once a week in a pleasant hall beside the local shopping centre in Dronfield. Like all groups set up by the Community Support Workers, two members of staff help to run the group. They also have a professional advisor to assist staff to sorted out any difficulties members are experiencing.

Members like:		
Talking	Sharing	Friendship
Mixing	The atmosphere	Looking forward
Getting out	Planning	The support
Understanding	Participating	Going on trips
Sharing celebrations		

Project Study

GOOD PRACTICE

Shared experience Members of the group feel a great deal of support through knowing that everybody in the group has shared a similar experience and can understand how they feel.

Mutual support Because of the common understanding shared by members, the group accepts a mutual support role; listening, caring and talking to each other when needed. Some members extend this beyond the group and telephone each other at home. Some members meet regularly for a because they have discovered they are near neighbours who hadn't met before joining the group.

Regularity As many of the group do not have the opportunity, or are unable to get out of the house much between meetings, the frequency of meetings is important. Being weekly, people enjoy anticipating the next meeting; it is never too far off.

Supported The group is very appreciative of the support and help they receive from the workers. Their role is seen as vital to the stability of the group as *"You need someone to take responsibility."* The workers also see themselves having a permanent role in the group; they can support individuals in the group, provide advice and prevent crisis from developing.

Facilitated not run Welcome though the workers are, the group has a strong regard for the rights of its members to decide matters for the group; *"The workers should be part of the group rather than an authority figure."*

Self-administrating Members are very careful to enable each other to participate in the running of the group. Monthly business meetings are held to plan the running of the group and although meetings are informal, officers have been appointed. A chairperson to *"make sure that everything is discussed and stop people talking when someone else is."* (Chair) and secretary to take. The notes are typed up and circulated to all members to keep them informed of what's going on and to keep a record. The benefit of the record is that it *"keeps your mind going to think about the group and to plan."*

Transport The group is very dependent on the staff to provided transport as public transport in NE Derbyshire is poor with a 5 or 6 mile journey taking up to one-and-a-half hours by bus. Taxis have had to be used on occasions but this is rare. Trips are usually made in cars—a mini-bus is occasionally hired. As the group meets beside a small shopping centre, some members take the opportunity to do some shopping while the meeting concludes so that they can get it home by car.

Project Study

Wider influence CONNECT is now sending a representative to a Local Planning Group. These planning groups have had a difficult history in the area and attempts are being made to renew interest in them and the effectiveness of them. As CONNECT is keen to have the voice of service users heard, the group is committed to having a member involved.

Coping with Change A major challenge CONNECT has had to cope with was the loss of its premises due to fire. Fortunately the outcome was a move to a nicer meeting room which is more relaxed, quiet and friendly. It also has easier wheelchair access.

The other major change some of the original members have felt very noticeably is in the size of the group. It has grown to its present 12 members over the years and people seemed to feel this is about the right size. This doesn't mean that it is closed to new people as it is used to members leaving for work, volunteering or to join another group. These changes are accepted, new members are welcomed even if their presence inevitably means change.

"Its sad to see people going away but its also good to see them move on." (Worker).

CONNECT is very important to its members. It provides much more than friendship; it provides a secure environment where concerns can be talked over with friends who have understanding. Members care for each other, are patient with each other's difficulties and take an interest in each other's news and knowledge. Trips out together are greatly enjoyed with the group breaking into smaller clusters of 3–4 people if they feel they are too big.

The semi-formal structure of the group ensures it runs smoothly, successfully enabling members to become involved in making decisions with and for the group and keeping members informed of what is going on.

Crucial to the group is the reassurance provided by the facilitators, the Community Support Workers. Their transportation is necessary but so is their participation in meetings. They link the group to wider sources of specialist help through the Killamarsh Mental Health Team, keep the momentum going if people are feeling unwell and help the group see their way through inevitable changes.

"We sort of seem very special to each other. I know there aren't many groups like us."

PROJECT STUDY

7

HOSTEL FOR THE HOMELESS

SOUTHFIELD HOSTEL IN THE SUMMER HILL COMPLEX, BIRMINGHAM.

Southfield is a hostel for single homeless people who are mentally ill, or have problems related to drug and substance abuse. It is run by Birmingham Social Services Department and forms part of the Summer Hill Complex for homeless people, sometimes known as the 'Roofless Project'. This is a city-wide service providing day care, accommodation, a specialist social work team and health care. Not only is it unique for its comprehensiveness but also for being open every day of the year and catering for as many as 250 people per day in winter.

The unusual feature of Summer Hill is it's high staffing levels of qualified social workers and its successful integration with health and housing. The Summer Hill Team includes 7 social workers with specialisms in welfare rights, alcohol and substance abuse and mental health. They work in close association with a primary health care service and a community mental health team who are located in the complex supporting both users of the day centre and residents of the associated accommodation.

In recognition of the recurring housing problems which are experienced by homeless people with mental health problems, the Summer Hill Team has developed three different supported housing schemes. Firstly, a block of 12 self-contained flats have been renovated, furnished and fitted with the co-operation of the Housing Department. These are let to people with long-term mental health problems and one flat has been converted into a community flat which is staffed between 9.00 am and 9.00 pm to provide a place where residents can meet together, get support and advice from the worker and have meals cooked for them. Secondly, 5 self-contained flats are rented from Shape Housing Project, furnished by the SSD to a high standard and let to tenants who are supported by Summer Hill staff. Their length of stay is variable depending on how quickly they are ready to move on to their own accommodation.

The third housing scheme is **Southfield Hostel**. It is situated a short distance from the Summer Hill Centre and is staffed 24 hours a day so providing a high level of support for residents and night cover for the supported flats. Two of the 12 bedrooms in the hostel are used for emergency accommodation.

Refurbished The hostel was opened in 1979 and completely refurbished in 1993/4 using capital raised in conjunction with the Mental Illness Specific Grant. No revenue funding was required as the staffing costs were being met prior to the refurbishment.

Project Study

Residents The hostel provides for male or female residents in single rooms. Access and facilities are available for wheelchair users. Although it is intended for adults over the age of 25, the hostel is sometimes used for emergency overnight accommodation for younger people, but every attempt is made to move them on to more appropriate accommodation the following morning.

Aims The aim of Southfield is to provide a good standard of short-term accommodation giving people a supported environment in which to regain health and stability. Individual needs are assessed and care plans are formulated and put into action, taking into account resident's short-term and long-term requirements.

"The emphasis will be on encouraging and developing user self awareness, self determination and self-control which would play a significant part in the ultimate rehabilitation programme." (Operational Policy, 6.12 1993)

Staff The hostel is staffed 24 hours a day with one waking and one sleeping member of staff present at night. A keyworker system operates and all residents are allocated to a social worker at Summer Hill. Domestic staff are responsible for cleaning the hostel and a part-time cook provides the meals when she is on duty. At other times the care staff have to take responsibility for meals and snacks. Residents are not able to use the kitchen.

Referrals Throughout the day, the Summer Hill Duty Team handles referrals but, after 5.00 pm, staff take referrals straight in from the emergency services including police and probation.

Activities The philosophy of the hostel is to provide support to enable residents to stand on their own feet. Staff will work with people involving them in activities, discussion groups, individual counselling, social skills training, outings and generally encouraging them to take part in the activities in the hostel.

Length of stay There is no time limit on stay at Southfield but 6 months is regarded as the optimum stay and a year the maximum length of residence. When people are ready, moving on is planned with built in safeguards for on-going support and after care.

Residents' likes   'Settled me down'   'Somewhere to go'   'Nice place'
                           'Good facilities'   'My own room'   'Friendly staff'
                           'Help to get better'   'The people here'

DILEMMAS

Staff shortage This prevents the keyworker system operating effectively and delays the implementation of care plans for individuals.

Frustration Residents experience frustration from the lack of activities in the hostel itself. This is due in part to staff shortages and in part to the wide mix of people living there coming from different cultural and ethnic backgrounds with differing ages, experience and needs. They may be recovering from mental illness, drug or solvent abuse or just need time and support to stabilise their lives before moving on to live independently. Also, Southfield takes in residents who have had difficulty fitting into other establishments.

GOOD PRACTICE

24 hour service Despite difficulties experienced through staff shortages, one of the hostel's main advantages is that it is staffed 24 hours a day. It can be used as a crisis house and provide an alternative to hospital admission.

Summer Hill The formal and informal links with Summer Hill extend the scope of the hostel considerably for residents. Staff also benefit from belonging to a larger staff group. This meets weekly at the Day Centre and providing a valuable source of support as well as an opportunity to share concerns.

Rehabilitation The staff do have success in helping people move on to a home of their own with appropriate support wherever possible. This may be in the existing supported housing schemes but these have such a low turnover, that further housing resources are being sought.

Flexibility The time it takes to prepare someone for independence and rent and furnish a house often exceeds the 6 months period a resident should stay in the hostel. Therefore, Southfield has had to adopt a flexible attitude to resident's length of stay.

Residents' Meetings These are held monthly and are attended by staff. Although some residents feel that the presence of the workers prevents open discussions, there seems to be doubt whether meetings would take place without staff intervention because of the very small number of residents at Southfield, 8 to 10 at any time and the shortness of their stay. Also, many residents don't feel well enough to take on responsibility for the meeting.

Advocacy Staff at Southfield find themselves working for their residents as advocates, both in keeping them at the hostel until they are ready to move on successfully and in securing the help they need.

"We can be an advocate for our residents. Everybody realises the difficulties we have down here. At one minute we are the best thing then the next we are the worst. Our reward is that we do have results."
(Worker)

Project Study

PROJECT STUDY

8

HOME BASED SERVICE FOR PEOPLE WITH DEMENTIA

THE EXTENDED COMMUNITY CARE SCHEME, SOUTHAMPTON

The Extended Community Care Scheme, or Companion Service, is a domiciliary support service for older people with dementia who live alone. It is the second community care service for people with dementia to be provided by Southampton MIND, the first being a Sitting Service offering breaks for carers. It was the demand for this service which led staff to research how people with dementia manage when they live on their own and to establish the need for a new innovative service. In 1991, a successful bid was made for MISG funding and, with start-up costs raised from the TVS Telethon, the Extended Community Care Scheme was ready to go into operation on the first day MISG was available.

The service The Extended Community Care Scheme aims to help people to live safely in their own homes for as long as possible by providing a 'companion' to befriend and support them. The companions are paid employees of MIND with training and experience of working with people who are confused and forgetful. They visit clients at agreed times, the regularity of visits depending on the individual needs of clients and the input of other services.

Staffing The two Community Care Schemes are managed by a full-time Director, Co-ordinator and secretary and two of the companions help out with the administration. There are 10 companions who are employed on a casual, part-time basis with no guaranteed minimum weekly hours of work. They each work independently but form two teams which meet fortnightly for supervision and mutual support. Individual support is also available as the service seeks to establish a strong cohesion between staff in order to offset the isolation and stress encountered with the work involved.

Location The catchment area for the service includes six social service districts in and around Southampton. The office is at the Harefield Day Hospital which is not only attended by many of the project's clients but is also a base for CPNs so enabling staff to keep in touch with both clients and health staff.

Advisory Group A multi-agency Advisory Group with representatives from health and social services also ensures the service remains aware of issues facing both agencies.

Criteria To qualify for the Companion Service a client must live alone in the catchment area, have a diagnosis of dementia made by a member of the medical staff of the local community mental health team and be subject to the care programme approach or have a care manager. This closed referral system has been introduced to ensure the companions are not the only service to whom the client is known. Often the help of other professionals is required and it has been found to be in the clients interest if multi-agency involvement is established early.

Key characteristics of the service:

Flexibility	Responsiveness to clients and carers
7 days a week	Informality
Free of charge	Co-operation with other services

GOOD PRACTICE

Gaining access The service has been very successful in gaining access into clients' homes; in the three and a half years the service has been running, access has only been refused twice.

"When we first go we get no acceptance and it can take a while to get accepted. Sometimes they keep you on the doorstep. You can't even get in but we still go back again and again and again. You gradually get inside the door but you have to stand up and then go. Then you might go back and have half an hour but you still don't sit down. Gradually you get in, you make a cup of tea and then you can talk. Then they don't let you out again. It's still nice, that." (Companion)

Flexibility Although companions visit for an agreed length of time so that they can plan their day, the service is flexible enough to allow variation to suit the individual requirements of the client. Visits are for a minimum of 1 hour but will be lengthened to enable the companion to go at the client's own pace.

Practical support In addition to providing emotional and social support, the companions give the practical support often ignored by other services which don't think through the implications of memory loss. For example, companions will encourage clients to eat their lunch from Meals-on-wheels as some confused people don't know what to do with the packaged meal they receive. Similarly, companions will collect prescriptions which have been left by a doctor or accompany clients to an out patients appointment to prevent them getting lost between the ambulance and the clinic.

Accepting risk Companions have become skilled at dealing with the mood swings which are often a feature of dementia and have had to learn to accept the risks which clients live with such as front doors left unlocked, toast being made on electric rings and drinking. The risk is carefully monitored and clients are supported in the community for as long as possible.

Project Study

Adjusting to loss Support is also given to clients and families if, and when, residential or nursing care is required but companions also find the loss of a client into a rest home traumatic as they can become more important than the family through their daily visits.

Carers The companions are greatly valued by members of client's families who often have difficulty accepting what is happening to their relative. Companions have got used to being placed in the middle where they *"help to sort out the tension between relative... calm it down and take the worry off them."* (Companion)

Complementary services Companions are very clear about where their tasks dovetail with those of other service and they will often pave the way for other services to come in. Once the companion has been accepted it is much easier to introduce another worker into the house such as a home care worker. Companions also encourage clients get out of the house to day care and will make sure they are dressed and ready for transport or even accompany them there.

Communication Because of the close working arrangements with other services, a Continuous Care Record has been developed to ease communication. This is kept in a client's home and is completed by each care worker who goes into the house. This is particularly helpful where complex care arrangements are in place and sometimes the record is used to leave messages for the client to read when they are alone.

CPA The CPA system is being used very successfully to support clients and the Companion Service is able to play an important role in the system. Before the introduction of CPA, social workers tended to assess the needs of clients, refer them to the Companion Service where relevant and then close the case if the service was satisfactorily introduced. This left the companions with a great deal of responsibility. Since the introduction of CPA, every client has a keyworker in the statutory sector who can be contacted by the Companion service if there are concerns. This has reduced the isolation felt by the project and has improved joint working to the benefit of the client. The Director contributes to all clients' CPA review meetings, sometimes with the companion, and keyworkers can be contacted directly by the companions on practical issues at any time.

Care management Another advantage of CPA in Hampshire is that it eases access to care management and therefore the care management budget. By applying to care managers for the cost of additional hours of support for clients when their condition deteriorates, the service has doubled its budget and the amount of support it can provide.

ISSUES

The following issues facing the service were raised by the staff:
- the need for an independent advocacy worker;
- the establishment of quality standards linked to a clear service agreement;
- clarity of the funding situation with MISG sitting alongside finance from spot contracts.

PROJECT STUDY

9

RESPITE CARE FOR PEOPLE LIVING WITH DEMENTIA

RESPITE CARE SCHEME FOR PEOPLE WITH DEMENTIA, CHESHIRE

The Respite Care for People with Dementia Scheme is a service of many parts which provides advice and support to carers and isolated older people who are experiencing dementia. Using volunteers, it provides a series of 'respite' group meetings and a home visiting service. In addition, the workers provide an information and support service. The project aims to work chiefly with people caring for a dementia sufferer but, as the needs of carers are often inextricably woven into the needs of the 'cared for', it meets the different, and combined, needs of both by taking a flexible approach to the ways in which clients choose to use the groups and visits.

The service   The Respite Care Scheme is based in CVS at Northwich and covers the Cheshire district of Vale Royal. It works in close association with the Alzheimer's Disease Society and the focus of the project is on the provision social and emotional support for carers through three Respite Care.

Funding   MISG is just one of a number of funding sources for the project which enable the service to be free to users, a small charge only being made for expenses such as transport, tea and coffee.

Staffing   The project is run by two part time workers, the Organiser and the Project Worker. The Organiser is on a three year contract working a 24 hour week in which she runs the weekly Respite Groups and the Alzheimer's Disease Society (ADS) monthly carers meeting, manages the visiting service, provides a telephone information and support service, assesses new referrals (34 January-September 1994) and recruits and trains volunteers.

Volunteers   Much of the hands-on service is provided by volunteers. About 15 volunteers provide the visiting service and a similar number support the group meetings. However, the turnover of volunteers, together with difficulties in recruitment, are giving cause for concern and the project is having to employ a care worker to ensure that its activities can be maintained.

Visiting service   The visiting service primarily aims to reduce the isolation experienced by carers and sufferers living with dementia. Visits by volunteers are usually weekly but less frequent contact is also maintained with clients who go into a nursing home and have difficulties settling. Volunteer visitors befriend and carry out light duties such as gardening, going out for tea and doing shopping but they may also help with more personal tasks such as taking a client to the doctor or chiropodist. Care is taken not to duplicate the work of other services. Stress is placed on the importance of volunteers reporting any concerns they have about their clients to the Organiser who will be responsible for contacting help as appropriate.

Respite Groups Two Respite Groups are up and running and a third one is being planned. They meet weekly in two different day centre premises in the evening. Transport to and from the group is provided. Initially, the groups were set up for the sufferers to enable the carer to have a break at home and but many of the carers preferred to get out themselves. They started to either come with the sufferer or to arrange for another member of their family to sit at home while they got out to the respite group.

"Some of the carers are isolated—they don't have a normal life and they see the respite group as their social evening." (Organiser)

Meetings are essentially social but carers do come with matters they want to discuss in private with the workers. Another room may be used for this, or a worker will arrange to visit someone at home.

Access to the service is very open with people learning about it through leaflets, publicity, friends, CPNs, social workers, other voluntary organisations and churches. The Organiser assesses all new referrals and may visit a number of times before any service is accepted. Once a client is know, contact is maintained for as long as it is wanted.

ADS Carers Meeting Once a month a carers' meeting is held which is run by the Organiser but funded by ADS. These meetings combine information exchange with social activities and provide valuable mutual support for carers.

Carers' likes	Friendship	Talking	The atmosphere
	A break	Understanding	Not alone
	Enjoyment	Information	The workers

GOOD PRACTICE

All welcome People attending the carers group and the respite groups understand the difficulties of caring for someone with dementia and, as a result, they welcome both carers, sufferers and ex-carers who continue to seek the support of the group even though they are freed from day to day caring responsibilities.

Listening One of the most important aspects of the group for carers is that they can be listened to, not necessarily by the whole group, but in small groups of friends and by the workers with assurance of confidentiality.

Project Study

Programme The Carers Group has a very varied programme which is set with the help of the members and arranged by the Organiser. It aims to find ways to help people let go and relax.

Keep in touch The Carers Group, together with the Respite Groups and support services, enables the staff to keep in touch with how people are, what difficulties are being encountered and where more help is needed. The workers get to know the clients so well that they are aware when circumstances are changing and are ready to provide additional support if possible. Key event, such as a sufferer having to be taken into a nursing home, will invariably trigger off the need for such support.

Support the family The service has always prioritised the need to reinforce the support being given within families. This may leave one person to bear the main responsibility, but complex support arrangements are found.

Involvement Members of the Carers Group are encouraged to become involved with the Alzheimer's Disease Society and two members have agreed to sit on the Committee.

ISSUES

Volunteer shortage Recent attempts at recruiting volunteers have been so unsuccessful the service is being forced to create a paid post for a care worker but there are fears that if all volunteers have to be replaced in this way, the nature of the service would change beyond recognition.

Expectations The shortage of volunteers, increases the pressure on the workers to deliver the service. The organiser already works well above her part-time hours and finds it difficult to restrict her day time activities to take account of her evening work.

Funding As with most voluntary sector projects, funding is an issue and clients are aware of the need to fund raise. They are willing to help with fund raising events but the responsibility for these once again falls to the staff. Despite these efforts, frustrations are felt by the financial constraints and uncertainties.

Lack of Recognition The Respite service may have a key role in the support of a client and yet the contribution made by the project and the judgement of the workers seems to go unrecognised by care managers. Social workers are slow to contact the project on request and workers are not invited to take part in care management reviews.

PROJECT STUDY

10

DAY CARE FOR OLDER PEOPLE IN A RURAL AREA

THE ACTIVITY BUS, SOMERSET

The Activity Bus provides day services for older people in West Somerset who have mental health problems. The focus for the project is a mini-bus with which the staff meet the challenge of providing support, stimulation and social contact to people living scattered throughout rural West Somerset by both taking the service to the people and by taking the people out into their beautiful countryside. However, the project provides much more than bus rides; the needs of carers are taken into account, people who are unable, or unwilling, to go out are visited at home and transport to key events is arranged so that clients can participate in local community activities.

Overall, the project aims to help people to live in their own homes for a long as possible, to prevent hospital admissions for mental health problems and to support people on discharge from hospital. It is run jointly by Somerset Social Services Department and the British Red Cross.

The Activity Bus project originated from the offer of a mini-bus by the Red Cross in Minehead, but behind the offer was the intention to provide transport for older people who were unable to travel in to social services day centres from rural villages and isolated locations. Recognising that a more innovative and stimulating approach would be to take the service to the people rather than to bring people in to a static service, a roving day service was planned and MISG secured.

Initially, the mini-bus was equipped with a table and a box of activities which could be set up in any suitable parking place once passengers had been collected from their scattered homes. Very soon it became apparent that this wasn't what clients wanted. They loved the bus, the people and the drivers but they didn't want the aboard-bus activities. There was enough to see and do simply driving around the lanes and by-ways of the area.

Location The bus covers the area of West Somerset and the office base is in the Minehead Social Services Offices.

Joint project Although the project is provided jointly by the Social Services Department and the British Red Cross, each agency has clear responsibilities. The service is managed by Somerset Social Services who employ and supervise the staff. The Red Cross taxes, insures and maintains the bus and recruits and trains volunteers.

The Activity Bus The bus is a 12 seater mini-bus with a tail lift and a high roof. To accommodate wheelchairs, and people with restricted mobility, the interior has been carefully adapted reducing the number

Project Study

of seats and increasing the space in which people can move around. It is equipped with emergency radio, first aid supplies, and, in summer, tables and chairs for outdoor coffee breaks.

Finance The running costs of the service are met by Social Services out of MISG. This funds two paid workers, the expenses and the Red Cross who charge 60 pence a mile for the use of the bus. The service was established with the expectation of supporting 25 clients a year but, although the number has doubled, no increase in funding has been negotiated. Therefore, the bus travel is now limited to 1000 miles a month, a distance easily covered in the extensive catchment area. The clients themselves help to fund tea and coffee and smaller expenses by paying £1 for every half day trip and £2 for full day trips. This contribution is willingly given.

Volunteers The bus drivers are volunteers who are trained by the Red Cross. There are 4 at present who give one day each. Volunteers also provide support on the bus and make home visits so freeing the workers and increasing the flexibility of the service. The volunteers attend team meetings and receive support from the project staff and manager.

The service The bus runs from Monday to Thursday, 9.15 am to 2.30 pm, with one worker and one volunteer on board. It picks people up from their home, however isolated , and then drives to wherever the passengers choose such as a favourite view-point, a place of general interest or a place of personal interest to one of the passengers. During the morning the bus stops for a coffee/tea break. Refreshments are carried on board so that those who don't want to get off the bus can sit comfortably in their seats while those who want to explore a bit, smoke or just have some fresh air can have the break outside. In hot weather clients are encouraged to sit out but in the winter they often call at hotels.

While the bus is out, the second worker catches up with administration, follows up referrals, carries out initial visits and provides home support. This work continues on Fridays when the bus is not in use.

Criteria The service is open to people of 65 and over who experience mental health problems. It supports clients who have depression, psychotic illness and dementia. The majority of referrals come from professionals, but referrals are accepted from anywhere. If a family refers someone, a check is made with the GP to ensure the appropriateness of the referral before an initial visit is made. These introductory visits are called 'Profile Visits'.

Users' likes	Social	Mix with different people	Gets you out
	All in the same boat	Talking	Get to know each other
	Looking forward to it	The support	Stimulation
	New interest	Reliability	All year round

GOOD PRACTICE

Choice The passengers choose where the bus goes each day once everybody has been picked up. This leads to lively discussions and encourages people to remember and reminisce. Each trip is an adventure, full of the unexpected, yet nothing more than sitting is required of the passengers. They don't even have to communicate; they will hear and see things and feel the movement of the bus

User centred One of the project's main priorities is finding out what is right for each individual who uses the service and this starts at the assessment or 'Profile Visit' but continues through all contacts. A bus ride may not be the answer; visits may be preferred or shopping trips.

Values the past Wherever possible, the workers and volunteers on the bus call on the knowledge and experience of the passengers. Each cross road and pub is an opportunity to share memories; the names are discussed to help orient people, changes are watched with interest, family connections are talked of.

Caring People on the bus have developed a very caring attitude towards each other. They accept they are not as all as fit as each others, and that somebody may feel very low some days.

Flexible The bus, together with outreach provided by car, gives an unusual amount of flexibility to the options offered to clients and carers. The bus is mainly used for the morning tours but it also caters for shopping trips, visits to each others houses and longer outings. Workers can even make home visits from the bus.

Professional The workers are selected for their personality and trained for the job. Although the project appears to be easy going, happy and casual, it has had to be professional in its approach and in the delivery of the service. As the Activity Bus is the only service many of its users have the workers are responsible for monitoring client's well being and reacting appropriately if there is cause for concern. Care is taken to record significant changes which are observed in clients and to pass this information on. As a result, good relationships have been developed with the back-up statutory services.

Project Study

ISSUES
- Frustration at the lack of perceived involvement of older people in Somerset in the planning and delivery of services despite the increasing demands from people with dementia and other mental health problems due to ageing.
- The dependence on a single source of funding which has not been increased since the service started is limiting the potential development of the project and giving rise to uncertainties about future sources of funding.

APPENDIX 1

METHODOLOGY

A1.1 Three sources of information were used for the 1993/4 National monitoring of MISG:
- the questionnaires sent to local authorities as part of the Department of Health circular inviting bids for the 1994/5 grant
- visits to 11 local authorities by the SSI
- a study of the views of MISG service users.

MISG SURVEY

A1.2 This aspect of the monitoring was undertaken between February and July 1994. The MISG Circular (LAC(94)6) contained a questionnaire to be completed by all local authorities. It was in two parts; the first covering expenditure on mental health services and the second requesting information about each project in receipt of MISG. Response to the survey was disappointing but, with reminders, a 74% response was obtained on the expenditure data and over 70% of local authorities returned information on MISG projects. The results are summarised in section 5 and additional tables are provided in Appendix 3 and 4.

SSI VISITS

A1.3 Ten local authorities were selected to be visited by a team of SSI staff. The authorities were chosen to provide a geographic spread throughout the country and a distribution of local authority type including metropolitan boroughs, shire counties and London boroughs. A further authority was selected for a pilot visit.

A1.4 The pilot visit was carried out in July 1994 and the visits were all completed by the end of August. A team of 2 or 3 inspectors made the visits which covered 2 or 3 days each. The aim of the visits was to assess the range, quality and effectiveness of services being provided by the grant and its overall impact. This was done through interviews, and group meetings, with key managers and practitioners, and visits to a number of MISG projects.

USERS' VIEWS

A1.5 After the visits by the SSI Team, one MISG project in each authority was chosen for the study of user views. The initial selection was made by the inspectors in discussion with the SSD, but this selection was refined by the independent researcher employed to carry out the study. The aim of the final selection was to ensure a range of projects were included representing some key characteristics of MISG projects such as:
- User type: -adult and older peoples' services
- Location: -rural and urban

- Type: -building and home based
- Sector: -statutory, voluntary and private
- Specialism: -black and ethnic minority
  -women's service
  -carers.

A1.6 Access was negotiated with each project separately. The researcher sent an information sheet about the study and herself (*including a photograph*) so that users could decide whether they wanted to participate in the study. It also enabled workers and users to know a little bit about the researcher before she arrived.

A1.7 Visits took place in 10 of the 11 authorities in the study. Where the project was a group which met regularly, the researcher attended a meeting (*3 cases*). If the service was in a building or meeting place, a day was spent with the project (*4 cases*). Where the service was home based, up to 2 days were spent with the project visiting users and talking with the staff (*3 projects*).

A1.8 The intention was to spend as much time talking to users as possible. This was done through group meetings, individual interviews and general participation in the activities of the project. Methods used included semi-structured interviews, a brief questionnaire and group work exercises. The method had to be adapted in each project to suit the circumstances, and the willingness and interest of the users taking part. Wherever possible, a tape recorder was used. In addition, the researcher tried to interview workers within the projects in order to understand the service more fully, and to be able to place users' comments in context.

A1.9 The most challenging situations were home based projects in which users could only be met in their own homes. In the short time available, it was not possible to set up individual interviews. Instead, respecting users' illness or dementia, the researcher accompanied the care workers on their normal visits and was introduced as a 'friend'. Where it was appropriate, the study was explained to the user, but this was not always possible. This experience was extremely useful in providing the researcher with a flavour of the work of the project concerned but, recognising that the primary aim of the home visit was support, discussions focused on the users' agenda, not that that of the research.

A1.10 After each visit, a report was prepared for the project to give participants an opportunity to see what was written. Only after their agreement, was the material used for this report.

APPENDIX 2

THE VISITS

A2.1　LOCAL AUTHORITIES

Pilot study:　Northamptonshire County Council

Visit programme, July and August 1994:
- Birmingham City Council
- Buckinghamshire County Council
- Cheshire County Council
- Derbyshire County Council
- Hampshire County Council
- Kirklees Metropolitan Borough Council
- London Borough of Redbridge
- London Borough of Sutton
- Salford City Council
- Somerset County Council

A2.2　MISG PROJECTS VISITED
- Activity Bus, Minehead, Somerset.
- Community Support Team, Milton Keynes
- Connect Group, North Derbyshire
- Extended Care Scheme, Southampton, Hampshire
- Mental Health Support Team, Salford
- New Commonwealth Women's Mental Health Project, Redbridge
- 'Rendezvous' Club 70, Batley, Kirklees
- Respite Care Scheme for People with Dementia, Northwich, Cheshire
- Southfield Hostel, Birmingham
- Wellington Street Day Centre, Northampton

APPENDIX 3

MISG ACTIVITY

This appendix should be read in conjunction with Section 5 of the report. It provides additional findings from the questionnaires sent to local authorities from the Department of Health as part of the package inviting bids for MISG in 1994/5. As response was patchy, the findings should be examined with care. In total information was supplied about 804 projects of an estimated 1,200 MISG projects nationally.

THE NATURE OF MISG PROJECTS

Method It is not easy to summarise the nature of the community mental health services funded by MISG. Not only does the wide range of services present problems for classification but also, because of the complexity of services offered, some projects could only accurately be classified in a number of groups. To take account of this, projects have been initially classified into 19 main groups but within each group, a further classification was made to more accurately describe of the types of projects MISG is funding.

Table A.1 Type of project by local authority type

Type of Project	County	IL	OL	MET	Total
Advocacy	17	4	6	7	34
Befriending	12	–	2	3	17
Carers	22	1	4	9	36
Crisis intervention	5	–	1	3	9
Day care	154	2	14	32	202
Drop-in	29	1	5	6	41
Employment	31	2	5	12	50
Home based	26	1	2	6	35
Homeless	7	1	1	2	11
Information	11	1	3	3	18
Leisure	7	–	2	–	9
MDO	5	–	–	–	5
MHT	126	1	10	34	171
Residential/housing	47	6	8	17	78
Respite/relief	16	–	3	4	23
Specialist budget	16	–	–	–	16
Training—staff	8	1	1	3	13
Training—users	10	–	–	4	14
Users projects	16	1	3	2	22
Total	565	22	70	147	804

Day Care The trend away from building based day services was apparent with only 39% of the 202 day care projects providing services in a day centre. A further 22 projects (11%) combined activities at a centre with outreach and 32 (16%) projects were outreach only. The 8 peripatetic services were mainly provided for older people to ensure services come as near to their homes as possible but this was not exclusively in rural areas. Other categories of services which contribute to day care services were mental health teams (MHT), home based services and drop-ins.

Figure A1: Types of Day Care

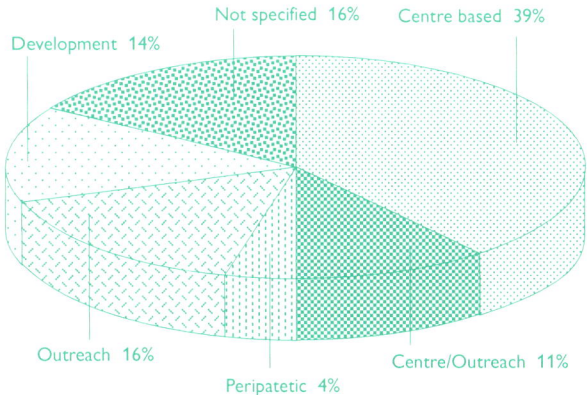

Figure A1: Types of Day Care
- Centre based 39%
- Not specified 16%
- Development 14%
- Outreach 16%
- Peripatetic 4%
- Centre/Outreach 11%

Mental Health Teams   MISG funds a range of activities and workers based in mental health teams (Fig. A2). The majority of professionals and specialists employed in these teams were social workers but many worked with specific groups of clients such as people with long-term mental health problems. Also based in MHTs were the 30 care management projects. Workers in MHTs with a remit to develop community outreach, day care opportunities, social support and training often had a similar role to workers in home based services.

Figure A2: MISG Investment in Mental Health Teams

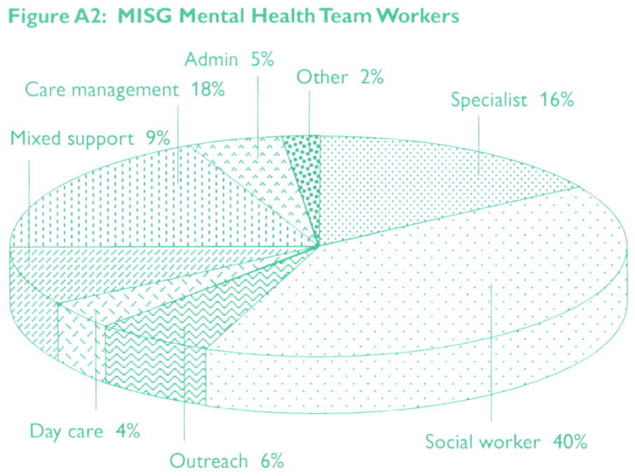

Figure A2: MISG Mental Health Team Workers
- Admin 5%
- Care management 18%
- Other 2%
- Mixed support 9%
- Specialist 16%
- Day care 4%
- Outreach 6%
- Social worker 40%

Residential/Housing   78 projects provide housing or residential provision and a further 10 projects provide specifically for people who are homeless. The housing projects largely provide supported accommodation including, supported housing, community living schemes, long stay residential projects, staged accommodation and adult placements (Fig.A3). 8 projects provide exclusively short stay and emergency accommodation.

Appendix

Homeless   3 of the 11 projects for people who are homeless and mentally ill are aimed at finding accommodation and a further 5 are involved in care management for this care group.

Figure A3: Types of Housing Projects

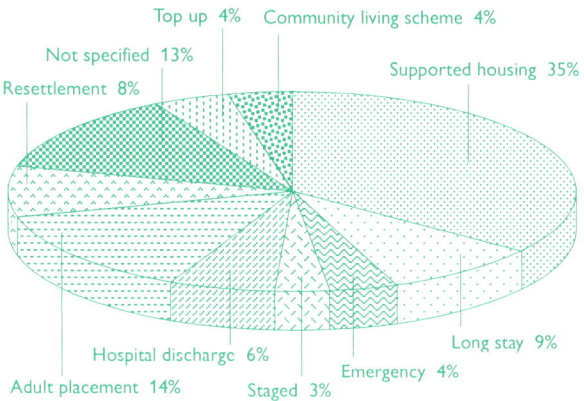

Figure A3: Types of Housing/Residential Schemes
- Top up 4%
- Community living scheme 4%
- Not specified 13%
- Supported housing 35%
- Resettlement 8%
- Hospital discharge 6%
- Long stay 9%
- Adult placement 14%
- Emergency 4%
- Staged 3%

Employment   Of the 50 employment projects, three quarters were involved in preparing people for work and only 10 (20%) actually provided employment.

Carers   Half of the 36 carers projects involved the provision of a support worker for carers. 12 other projects provided 'relief' for carers. This was all home based, half of the services involving a night carer.

Respite and relief care   An additional 23 projects were described as providing 'respite and relief' but this could be for both carers and the service user. 14 of these projects were sitting services and 3 involved activities in a centre.

Drop-in   8 of the 41 drop-in projects were run by service users or were intended to provided mutual support. 15 (37%) were informal or unstructured drop-ins and a further third were more structured, providing groups and activities.

Home based   Over half of the 35 projects involved domiciliary care and a further 12 (34%) focused on providing practical support, often skills training at home. Two projects provided aftercare support following discharge from hospital.

Advocacy Services   Of the 34 advocacy projects, 10 were providing training to potential advocates or were publishing advocacy services. 3 projects focused on advocacy in care management and 5 in relation to welfare benefits. In two projects, advocacy was provided for a mixed group of service users rather than just mental health users.

User Projects This category includes projects which were described as being run by service users. 18 were self help projects and 3 were dedicated to obtaining the views of service users usually for planning or evaluation purposes.

Information 15 (88%) of projects were providing users with information about health issues. Two specifically mentioned publicity and some aim to inform carers and professionals in addition to users.

Befriending 14 befriending projects were for general social contact, none offered an out of hours service.

Specialist management schemes 16 projects involve the use of small budgets for ad hoc purposes. Examples of the use of these budgets included fees for training courses, materials, child care to enable users to attend group sessions, equipment needed by users to participate in day care activities. Some authorities describe a number of small special budgets under £10k.

Training There were two aspects of training, firstly training for service users and secondly for staff. Training for users focused on skills training which was also provided in some day centres and by some home support teams. 6 projects were particularly concerned with professional training for staff and one with race training. Included in this group are 7 projects involved in the training for, or general aspects of, service development.

Leisure 9 projects involved leisure activities but no details were given.

Crisis Intervention 9 projects were described as offering crisis intervention, 2 of which involved multidisciplinary assessment.

Mentally Disordered Offenders Only 5 specific projects were listed for mentally disordered offenders. One was a diversion scheme and one a research and development project but no other information was available.

ADDITIONAL TABLES FROM THE SURVEY

Table A.2 Rank order of objectives/outcomes of projects

Objective	No. of Projects	% of Total
Relief care and support	136	17
Stimulating safe environment	101	13
Enhancing user choice	80	10
Accommodation opportunities	64	8
Support—social/emotional	61	8
Care management	54	7
Preparation for work	52	7
Reduce hospital admission	39	5
Rehabilitation	36	5
User empowerment	36	5
Support—practical	32	4
Keep in touch with the community	17	2
Develop support networks	14	2
Skills training for service users	13	2
Skills training for staff	12	2
Support—domestic	10	1
Facilitating hospital discharge	10	1
Administrative support	9	1
Support—mutual	7	1
Promote mental health awareness	7	1
Develop interagency networks	7	1
Maintain contact/tracking	2	0.2
Capital/building	1	0.1
Not specified	4	1
Total	804	100.0

Table A.3 Target group for projects for people under the age of 65 by local authority type

Target Group	County	IL	OL	METS
Severely MI in the community	355	18	43	94
Carers	167	4	18	51
Black and minority ethnic people	112	7	40	59
Resettled from long stay hospital	146	3	23	32
Homeless people	98	3	16	36
Mentally disordered offenders	86	1	13	34
Other groups	66	4	1	14

Table A.4 People over 65 to whom MISG projects are targeted by local authority type.

Target Group	County	IL	OL	METS
Severely MI in the community	205	1	30	46
Carers	122	1	19	27
Black and minority ethnic people	26	2	18	9
Resettled from long stay hospital	40	–	5	4
Homeless people	11	–	3	1
Mentally disordered offenders	–	–	1	–
Other groups	25	–	–	4

Table A.5 Number of service users under 65 by local authority type.

Type of Project	County	IL	OL	MET	Totals
Severely MI in the community	21,842	592	3,236	5,455	31,125
Carers	4,560	66	250	1,331	6,207
Black and minority ethnic people	2,684	549	1,295	1,514	6,042
Resettled from long stay hospital	4,070	37	570	1,085	5,762
Homeless people	2,892	88	356	1,053	4,389
Mentally disordered offenders	701	30	143	178	1,052
Other groups*	3,891	426	30	1,064	5,411

Table A.6 Number of service users over 65 by local authority type.

Type of Project	County	IL	OL	MET	Totals
Severely MI in the community	12,576	220	1,090	5,485	19,371
Carers	5,575	16	861	1,814	8,266
Black and minority ethnic people	111	86	168	139	504
Resettled from long stay hospital	404	–	71	30	505
Homeless people	47	–	8	76	71
Mentally disordered offenders	–	–	5	–	5
Other groups*	1,105	–	–	48	1,153

* Other groups include under 25s, families, single parents, persons in crisis, older people in residential care or nursing homes, people with learning difficulties and children of women with post natal depression.

Appendix

APPENDIX 4

MISG EXPENDITURE

Introduction This appendix provides more detailed expenditure information than the text of Section 5. The response from local authorities was patchy and findings should be examined with care.

Table A7 shows the total amount of MISG payments (i.e. the 70% central government contribution) made to local authorities in the financial year ending 31st March 1994, including reallocated money.

Table A.7 Total Central Government MISG payments to all local authorities, 1993/4

LA Type	Amount (£000s)	Percentage of Total
Counties	17502.14	52.9
Inner London	3634.09	11.0
Outer London	3736.29	11.3
Mets	8205.36	24.8
Total	33077.88	100.0

Table A8 shows how much of the 70% MISG allocation had been taken up by the 31st March 1994.

Table A8 : Amount of 70% MISG allocation spent by local authorities by 31st March 1994 (based on responses of 80 LAs only)

LA Type	Amount (£000s)
Counties	12567.73
Inner London	432.91
Outer London	2331.38
Mets	8145.19
Total	23477.21

Revenue Expenditure Tables A9, A10 and A11 give the actual/estimated gross revenue expenditure by SSDs on specialist services for the mentally ill for the financial years 1992/3 and 1993/4.

Table A9 : Actual/estimated gross revenue expenditure by local authorities, 1992/3

Management Category	MISG 70%	30%	(£000s) Total	Other (£000s)	Total (£000s)
SSD	12947.15	5701.41	18648.56	31621.07	50269.63
SSD/Health joint	814.78	366.01	1180.79	1784.66	2965.45
Vol. Sector	5349.27	2228.45	7577.72	4358.37	11936.09
Private Sector	129.74	54.31	184.05	6.00	190.05
Other	81.76	29.76	111.52	1095.89	1207.41
Totals	19322.70	8379.94	27702.64	38865.99	66568.63

Table A10 : Actual/estimated gross revenue expenditure by local authorities, 1993/4

Management Category	MISG 70%	30%	(£000s) Total	Other (£000s)	Total (£000s)
SSD	12947.15	5701.41	18648.56	31621.07	50269.63
SSD/Health joint	814.78	366.01	1180.79	1784.66	2965.45
SSD	15090.39	6622.57	21712.96	33044.27	55516.22
SSD/Health joint	1122.17	524.58	1646.75	2162.69	3891.44
Vol. Sector	6183.95	2496.20	8680.15	8415.74	17186.88
Private Sector	120.05	51.45	171.50	923.59	1095.09
Other	81.53	38.50	120.03	774.76	894.79
Totals	22598.09	9733.30	32331.39	45321.05	78584.42

NB: Totals included in the right-hand column of the above table include some amounts not specified in the 'MISG' or 'Other' columns.

Table A11: Comparison of total gross local authority expenditure on services for the mentally ill, 1992/3 and 1993/4 by amount and percentage.

Management Category	1992/3 £(000s)	%	1993/4 £(000s)	%
SSD	50269.63	76	55516.22	71
SSD/Health joint	2965.45	4	3891.44	5
Vol. Sector	11936.09	18	17186.88	22
Private Sector	190.05	0.2	1095.09	1
Other	1207.41	2	894.79	1
Totals	66568.63	100	78584.42	100

The above table shows that there was an 18% increase in overall expenditure on services for mentally ill people by those authorities providing information. It should be noted, however, that this information is based on a response from around three-quarters of authorities, that no correction has been made for inflation, and that 27% of the increase is attributable to the 70% contribution to MISG made by the central government. The figure shows that 73% of the

£12 million overall increase was provided from sources other than the central government's contribution to MISG, not allowing for inflation.

30% contribution Information was provided (Table A12) about the source of the 30% local contribution authorities were required to make under the terms of MISG.

Table A12 :   Source of MISG 30% contribution, 1992/3 and 1993/4

Source	1992/3		1993/4	
	Amount	%	Amount	%
SSD base budget	6972.49	84	8476.13	84
Joint finance	1231.55	15	1386.91	14
Other	110.98	1	193.66	2
Total	8315.02	100	10056.70	100

APPENDIX

5

BIBLIOGRAPHY

Audit Commission (1986) *Making a Reality of Community Care*, London: HMSO.

Barnes, D. (Ed) (1992) 'The North's Response to MISG' in *Fighting fires with a Short Hosepipe: The impact of the Mental Illness Specific Grant*, Durham: Northern Regional Health Authority and Institute of Health Studies, University of Durham.

Barnes, D. (1993) *MISG in the North 1991/3: A directory of community mental health projects*, Durham: Institute of Health Studies, University of Durham.

Barnes, D. (1994) 'The impact of the Mental Illness Specific Grant in the Northern Region', *Practice*, 7(1), pp.19-30.

Coia, D.A. McKillop, A. and McCreadle, G.G. (1994) 'The Mental Illness Specific Grant in Scotland', *Psychiatric Bulletin*, March, 18(3), pp143-147.

Cobb, A. (1990) 'After all those promises', *OPENMIND*, 47, pp5.

Day, S. (1991) 'New money for new services? How the MISG will be spent', *South West MIND Newsletter*, pp3.

Department of Health and Social Security (1975) *Better Services for the Mentally Ill*, London: HMSO.

Department of Health (1989) *Caring for People: Community Care in the Next Decade and Beyond*, London: HMSO.

Department of Health (1990a) *Community Care in the Next Decade and Beyond: Policy Guidance*, London: HMSO.

Department of Health (1990b) *Specific grant for the development of social care services for people with a mental illness*, Circular HC(90)24; LAC(90)10, London: Department of Health.

Department of Health (1991a) *Community Care: Services for People with a Mental Handicap and People with a Mental Illness*, Government Response to the Eleventh Report from the Social Services Committee Session 1989-90, London: HMSO.

Department of Health (1991b) *People with a mental illness: local authority specific grant for 1992/3*, Health Service Guidelines HSG(91)23, London: Department of Health.

Department of Health (1991c) *Specific grant for the development of social care services for people with a mental illness*, Circular LAC(91)19, London: Department of Health.

Department of Health (1991d) *Mental Illness specific Grant Increased by nearly 50 percent*, Press Release H91/610, London: Department of Health.

Department of Health (1992) *The Health of the Nation: a strategy for health in England*, London: HMSO.

Department of Health (1994a) *Community Care Monitoring: Special Study: Mental Health Services*, London: Department of Health.

Department of Health (1994b) *Specific Grant for the development of social care services for people with a mental illness*, Circular LAC(94)6 and accompanying health guidance HSG(94)6, London: Department of Health.

Department of Health and Home Office (1992) *Review of health and social services for mentally disordered offenders and others requiring similar services* (The Reed Review), London: HMSO.

Department of Health Social Services Inspectorate (1992) *Mental illness specific grant: monitoring of proposals for use 1991/2*, London: HMSO

Department of Health Social Services Inspectorate (1993a) Mental Illness Specific Grant: second report on monitoring its use 1991/2, London: HMSO.

Department of Health Social Services Inspectorate (1993b) *Inspection of projects funded by the Mental Illness Specific Grant*, London: HMSO.

Foster, T.A. (1991) *Association of Directors of Social Services, Study of Future Requirements for the Mental Illness Specific Grant*, (unpublished).

Good Practices in Mental Health and SSI (1993) *Working Together for Mental Health*, London: Good Practices in Mental Health.

Griffiths, Sir Roy (1988) *Community Care: Agenda for Action*, London: HMSO.

Groves, T. (1991) 'The mental illness grant: Too little, too soon', *British Medical Journal*, 302, 15 June, pp1416-7.

Hansard (1989) Vol 156, 12 and 13 July, pp622-627.

Hogman, G. and Westall, J. (1991) *The Mental Illness Specific Grant; the early days*, Kingston-upon-Thames: National Schizophrenia Fellowship.

Hogman, G. (1992) *Window Dressing*, Kingston-upon-Thames: National Schizophrenia Fellowship.

House of Commons (1985) *Second report from the Social Services Committee on Community Care with special reference to adult mentally ill and mentally handicapped people*, London: HMSO.

Hudson, B. (1990) 'Looking for a way out'. *Health Service Journal*, 100 (5219), pp1354-5.

Ivory, M. (1992) 'Councils raid clients' cash to fund grants.' *Community Care*, 2 April, pp2.

May, A. (1989) 'Community Care: more questions than answers'. *Health Service Journal*, 99 (5173), pp1272.

Social Services Inspectorate (1991) *Community care in the West Midlands. Caring for people Seminar 30 January 1991: Specific grant for the development of social care for people with a mental illness*, Birmingham: SSI Central Region.

Social Services Inspectorate (1993) *Inspection of services funded by Mental Illness Specific Grant in Hereford and Worcester,* Birmingham: SSI Central Region.

Social Services Inspectorate (1993) *Inspection of projects funded by the Mental Illness Specific Grant in Humberside,* Gateshead: SSI Northern Region.

Social Services Inspectorate (1993) *Inspection of projects funded by the Mental Illness Specific Grant in Dorset,* Bristol: SSI South West Region.